Alistai

X

Bloomsbury Methuen Drama
An imprint of Bloomsbury Publishing Plc

B L O O M S B U R Y
LONDON · OXFORD · NEW YORK · NEW DELHI · SYDNEY

Bloomsbury Methuen Drama

An imprint of Bloomsbury Publishing Plc

Imprint previously known as Methuen Drama

50 Bedford Square	1385 Broadway
London	New York
WC1B 3DP	NY 10018
UK	USA

www.bloomsbury.com

Bloomsbury is a registered trade mark of Bloomsbury Publishing Plc

First published 2016

© Alistair McDowall 2016

British Library Cataloguing-in-Publication Data
A catalogue record for this book is available from the British Library.

ISBN: PB: 978-1-3500-0462-7
EPDF: 978-1-3500-0463-4
EPUB: 978-1-3500-0464-1

Library of Congress Cataloging-in-Publication Data
A catalog record for this book is available from the Library of Congress.

Typeset by Mark Heslington Ltd, Scarborough, North Yorkshire

THE ROYAL COURT THEATRE
PRESENTS

X

by Alistair McDowall

X was first performed at the Royal Court Jerwood Theatre Downstairs,
Sloane Square, on Wednesday 30 March 2016.

X

by Alistair McDowall

CAST (in alphabetical order)

Cole **Rudi Dharmalingam**
Young Mattie **Grace Doherty**
Ray **Darrell D'Silva**
Young Mattie **Amber Fernée**
Clark **James Harkness**
Gilda **Jessica Raine**
Mattie **Ria Zmitrowicz**

Director **Vicky Featherstone**
Designer **Merle Hensel**
Lighting Designer **Lee Curran**
Composer & Sound Designer **Nick Powell**
Video Designer **Tal Rosner**
Casting Director **Amy Ball**
Assistant Director **Roy Alexander Weise**
Associate Designer **Moi Tran**
Production Manager **Matt Noddings**
Costume Supervisor **Lucy Walshaw**
Fight Director **Bret Yount**
Stage Manager **Sunita Hinduja**
Deputy Stage Manager **Nicki Barry**
Assistant Stage Manger **Heather Cryan**
Stage Management Work Placement **Jodell Hill**
Chaperone **Tanya Shields**
Set Construction & Painting by **Belgrade Production Services**

The Royal Court & Stage Management wish to thank the following for their help on this production:
The Jerwood Space

y Alistair McDowall

listair McDowall (Writer)

r the Royal Court: **Talk Show** (Open Court).

her theatre includes: **Pomona (Orange Tree/ ational/Royal Exchange, Manchester); Brilliant dventures (Royal Exchange, Manchester/ ve Theatre); Captain Amazing (Live Theatre/ dinburgh Festival Fringe/tour).**

ee Curran (Lighting Designer)

r the Royal Court: **Linda, Constellations.**

ther theatre includes: **Doctor Faustus, Love's acrifice, Arden of Faversham (RSC); Splendour Donmar); The Oresteia (Home, Manchester); lamlet, Much Ado About Nothing, Blindsided Royal Exchange, Manchester); A Number Nuffield/Young Vic); Mametz (National Theatre Wales); Protest Song (National); Turfed, 66 Minutes in Damascus (LIFT); Regeneration, ancing at Lughnasa (Royal & Derngate, Northampton); Blam! (Neander); The Sacred Iame (ETT/Rose, Kingston); The Fat Girl Gets a Iaircut & Other Stories, Puffball (Roundhouse); Clytemnestra (Sherman Cymru); The Rise & Shine of Comrade Fiasco, Unbroken (Gate); The Empty Quarter (Hampstead).**

Dance includes: **Sun, Political Mother, The Art of Not Looking Back, In Your Rooms, Uprising (Hofesh Shechter); Untouchable (The Royal Ballet); Frames, Curious Conscience (Rambert Dance Company); The Measures Taken, All That Is Solid Melts into Air, The Grit in the Oyster (Alexander Whitley); Bastard Amber, Interloper (Liz Roche); There We Have Been (James Cousins).**

Opera includes: **Orpheé et Eurydice (ROH); Ottone, Life on the Moon (ETO); Nabucco (Opera National de Lorraine).**

Rudi Dharmalingam (Cole)

For the Royal Court: **Hope.**

Theatre includes: **Hamlet (Barbican); Oresteia (Almeida); Worst Wedding Ever (Salisbury Playhouse); The Events (Young Vic/UK tour); The Seagull (Headlong/UK Tour); Much Ado About Nothing (RSC/West End); You Can Still Make a Killing (NT Studio); Dara, England People Very Nice, Playing with Fire (National); Rafta Rafta (National/UK Tour); The English Game (Headlong); The Fastest Clock in the Universe (Naach); The History Boys (National/Broadway/ international tour); The Geri Project (Oldham Coliseum); The Tempest, Anorak of Fire (Adelphi Studio); Tom's Midnight Garden (Unicorn).**

Television: **Casualty, Doctor Who, Coronation Street, Hollyoaks, New Tricks, The Bill, Cutting It.**

Film includes: **Britz, Hamlet at the Barbican (NT Live).**

Radio includes: **The Events, Tommies, Love Lies Sleeping (Baccaccio's Decameron), The Shape of Things.**

Grace Doherty (Young Mattie)

Theatre includes: **Made in Dagenham (West End).**

Television includes: **Casualty.**

Darrell D'Silva (Ray)

For the Royal Court: **The Lying Kind.**

Other theatre includes: **Wendy & Peter Pan, Little Eagles, Antony & Cleopatra, King Lear, Julius Caesar, The Drunks, The Winter's Tale, Hecuba, A Midsummer Night's Dream, A Month in the Country, Troilus & Cressida, Camino Real, The Spanish Tragedy, Henry VIII, Doctor Faustus (RSC); Dunsinane (RSC/National Theatre of Scotland/World Tour); Making Stalin Laugh (JW3); Public Enemy, Six Characters in Search for An Author (Young Vic); Hedda Gabler (Old Vic); Children's Children (Almeida); Paradise Lost (Theatre Royal, Northampton); Closer, Tales from Vienna Woods, The Rose Tattoo, The Royal Hunt of the Sun (National); Absolutely! (Perhaps) (West End); The White Devil (Menier Chocolate Factory); Fall (Traverse); Clouds (UK Tour); Tear from a Glass Eye (Gate); Romeo & Juliet, The Three Musketeers (Crucible Sheffield); Further than the Furthest Thing (Tron); Crossfire (Plaines Plough); Chasing the Moment (One Tree).**

Television includes: **Endeavour III, Asylum, Father Brown, Top Boy 2, The Minor Character, Trial & Retribution, Bonekickers, Criminal Justice, Unsinkable Titanic, A Very British Sex Scandal, Poppy Shakespeare, First New Heart, Saddam's Tribe, To Be First, Krakatoa, Eleventh Hour, Spooks, Lawless, Messiah, Cambridge Spies, Dinotopia, Table Twelve: After Hours, Queen of Swords, The Bill, In Defence, Out of the Blue, Woken Well, Prime Suspect, Faith.**

Film includes: **The Throwaways, Alan Moore's & Mitch Jenkins' Show Pieces, Northmen: A Viking Saga, Montana, Closer to the Moon, Dirty Pretty Things.**

Radio includes: **Doctor Zhivago, A Suit of Lights, Cry Wolf, A Game of Three Halves.**

Vicky Featherstone (Director)

For the Royal Court: **Cyprus Avenue (& Abbey), How To Hold Your Breath, God Bless the Child, Maidan: Voices from the Uprising, The Mistress Contract, The Ritual Slaughter of Gorge Mastromas; Untitled Matriarch Play, The President Has Come to See You (Open Court Weekly Rep).**

Other theatre includes: **Our Ladies of Perpetual Succour, Enquirer (co-director), An Appointment with the Wicker Man, 27, The Wheel, Somersaults, Wall of Death: A Way of Life (co-director), The Miracle Man, Empty, Long Gone Lonesome (National Theatre of Scotland); Cockroach (National Theatre of Scotland/ Traverse); 365 (National Theatre of Scotland/**

Edinburgh International Festival); Mary Stuart (National Theatre of Scotland/Citizens/Royal Lyceum, Edinburgh); The Wolves in the Walls (co-director) (National Theatre of Scotland/Tramway/Lyric, Hammersmith/UK tour/New Victory, New York); The Small Things, Pyrenees, On Blindness, The Drowned World, Tiny Dynamite, Crazy Gary's Mobile Disco, Splendour, Riddance, The Cosmonaut's Last Message to the Woman He Once Loved in the Former Soviet Union, Crave (Paines Plough).

Television Includes: Where the Heart Is, Silent Witness.

Vicky was Artistic Director of Paines Plough 1997-2005 and the inaugural Artistic Director of the National Theatre of Scotland 2005-2012. Vicky is the Artistic Director of the Royal Court.

Amber Fernée (Young Mattie)

Theatre includes: Ballyturk (National).

Television includes: Penny Dreadful, Witch Hunt, The Living & the Dead.

James Harkness (Clark)

Theatre includes: The Absence of War (Crucible Sheffield); Great Britain (National/West End); Nighthawkes (Citizens); Blackout (National).

Television includes: One of Us, Moving On, Silent Witness, River City.

Film includes: Macbeth, The Program, Hector, Winter.

Merle Hensel (Designer)

For the Royal Court: The Mistress Contract.

Other theatre includes: Macbeth (costumes only) (Young Vic); Arden of Faversham (RSC); Much Ado About Nothing (Royal Exchange, Manchester); Protest Song (National); Macbeth (National Theatre of Scotland/Lincoln Center/Broadway/Japanese Tour); Green Snake (National Theatre of China); Glasgow Girls, 27, The Wheel (National Theatre of Scotland); The Shawl, Parallel Elektra (Young Vic); Shun-kin (Complicité); The Girls of Slender Means (Stellar Quines); Diener Zweier Herren (Schlosstheater Vienna); Ippolit (Sophiensaele, Berlin/Schauspielhaus Zürich/Münchner Kammerspiele); Der Verlorene (Sophiensaele, Berlin); Kupsch (Deutsches Theater, Göttingen).

Dance includes: The Barbarians in Love (costumes only), The Good/We Know, Sun, Political Mother (Hofesh Schechter); Lovesong (Frantic Assembly); James Son of James, The Bull, The Flowerbed (Fabulous Beast Dance Theatre); Justitia, Park (Jasmin Vardimon Dance Company/Peacock/International tour); Human Shadows (Underground7/The Place Prize).

Opera includes: Maria Stuarda (Vereinigte Bühnen, Mönchengladbach/Krefeld); Der Vetter Aus Dingsda (Oper Graz); Lunatics (Kunstfest Weimar); Münchhausen, Herr Der Lügen (Neuköllner Oper, Berlin).

Film includes: Morituri Te Salutant, Baby.

Merle Hensel works internationally in a wide variety of styles and genres. She is also a lecturer at Central St Martins School of Art and Design in London. Other teaching includes Rose Bruford College and Goldsmiths.

Nick Powell (Composer & Sound Designer)

For the Royal Court: The Mistress Contract, The Ritual Slaughter of Gorge Mastromas, Narrative, Get Santa! (co-creator), The Vertical Hour, The Priory, Relocated, The Nether (& West End); Talk Show (Open Court).

Other theatre includes: The Haunting of Hill House (Liverpool Everyman & Playhouse); Lord of the Flies (UK tour); Lanark: A Life in Three Acts (Citizens/Royal Lyceum, Edinburgh); Peter Pan, All My Sons, Lord of the Flies, The Crucible (Regent's Park Open Air); Wolf Hall/Bring Up the Bodies (RSC/West End/Broadway); The King's Speech (Chichester Festival); Dunsinane (National Theatre of Scotland/RSC/UK & US tours); Of Mice & Men (Birmingham Rep/tour); Show 6 - Secret Theatre (Lyric, Hammersmith/Edinburgh Fringe Festival); Othello (National); A Life of Galileo, Richard III, The Drunks, God in Ruins (RSC); Los Macbez (CDN Madrid); Bank on It (Theatre Rites); 'Tis Pity She's a Whore (Cheek by Jowl); 27, The Wheel, The Wonderful World of Dissocia (National Theatre of Scotland); Urtain, Marat-Sade (CDN Madrid/Animalario); Paradise (Rhur Triennale/Theatre Rites); Penumbra, Tito Andronico (Animalario, Madrid); The Danton Affair (Stadsteater Gothenburg); Panic (Improbable); The Family Reunion (Donmar); Realism (Edinburgh International Festival/National Theatre of Scotland); The Wolves in the Walls (National Theatre of Scotland/Tramway/Lyric, Hammersmith/UK tour/New Victory, New York).

Nick also writes extensively for TV & film. He is half of OSKAR who have released two albums and produced installations for the V&A and CCA, as well as written live soundtracks for Prada in Milan.

Jessica Raine (Gilda)

Theatre includes: Roots (Donmar); The Changeling (Young Vic); Rocket to the Moon, Earthquakes in London, Gethsemane, Harper Regan (National); Ghosts (West End); Punk Rock (Lyric, Hammersmith/Royal Exchange, Manchester).

Television includes: Inside No. 9, Jericho, Partners in Crime, Wolf Hall, Fortitude, Call the Midwife, Line of Duty, An Adventure in Space & Time, Doctor Who, Garrow's Law.

Film includes: The Woman in Black, Robin Hood.

Tal Rosner (Video Designer)

For the Royal Court: You For Me For You.

Theatre includes: Everyman, Husbands & Sons (National); The Four Fridas (Greenwich & Docklands Festival).

Dance includes: The Most Incredible Thing,

mpass (Sadler's Wells); Fold Here (Jerwood undation, Montclair Peak Performances); ertia (Channel 4 Random Acts).

rchestral music includes: **Four Sea Interludes & assacaglia** by Benjamin Britten (BBC Symphony rchestra/Miami New World Symphony/San rancisco Symphony/Philadelphia Orchestra/ os Angeles Philharmonic); **In Seven Days** iano Concerto with Moving Image by Thomas dès & Tal Rosner (Southbank Centre/London nfonietta/Los Angeles Philharmonic/New York hilharmonic).

hamber music includes: **Bilder aus Osten** by Robert chumann (for Katia & Marielle Labeque/ usseldorf Festival); **Lachen Verlernt** by sa-Pekka Salonen (for Jennifer Koh at berlin Conservatory/92nd Street Y/Carolina erforming Arts/TriBeCa Film Festival).

elevision includes: **Dates, Skins.**

wards include: **BAFTA** for Best Title Sequence Skins).

al has designed commercial videos for Louis uitton, Dior, Chanel and Sony Bravia. He has lso designed video for The Great North Run Million Opening Ceremony in Newcastle, 2014.

Roy Alexander Weise (Assistant Director)

As Director, for the Royal Court: **In Smoke, Aperture (Live Lunch).**

As Assistant Director, for the Royal Court: **Escaped Alone, You For Me For You, Hangmen, Primetime 2015, Violence & Son, Who Cares, Liberian Girl.**

As Director, other theatre includes: **Plunder, One Million Tiny Plays about Britain** (Young Vic); **Palindrome** (Miniaturists at Arcola); **The Man in the Green Jacket** (Jermyn Street); **What Happens Behind the Bar** (Cockpit); **SKEEN!** (Ovalhouse); **Invisible Mice** (Lyric, Hammersmith); **Seventeen** (Rose Bruford College); **Chameleon** (Unicorn).

As Assistant Director, other theatre includes: **Albion, We Are Proud to Present...**(Bush); **Public Enemy, Hamlet, The Government Inspector** (Young Vic); **The Serpent's Tooth** (Shoreditch Town Hall/ Almeida/Talawa); **Lulu** (Rose Bruford College).

Roy is currently the Trainee Director at the Royal Court Theatre.

Ria Zmitrowicz (Mattie)

Theatre includes: **Four Minutes Twelve Seconds** (Hampstead/Trafalgar Studios); **The Crucible** (Royal Exchange, Manchester); **Arcadia** (ETT); **God's Property** (Soho); **Chapel Street** (Bush/Old Vic New Voices/Old Red Lion).

Television includes: **Mr Selfridge, Youngers, Nightshift, The Midnight Beast, Casualty, Murder on the Home Front, Whitechapel.**

Film includes: **Kill Your Friends.**

THE ROYAL COURT THEATRE

The Royal Court Theatre is the writers' theatre. It is the leading force in world theatre for energetically cultivating writers – undiscovered, new and established.

Through the writers the Royal Court is at the forefront of creating restless, alert, provocative theatre about now, inspiring audiences and influencing future writers. Through the writers the Royal Court strives to constantly reinvent the theatre ecology, creating theatre for everyone.

We invite and enable conversation and debate, allowing writers and their ideas to reach and resonate beyond the stage, and the public to share in the thinking.

Over 120,000 people visit the Royal Court in Sloane Square, London, each year and many thousands more see our work elsewhere through transfers to the West End and New York, national and international tours, residencies across London and site-specific work.

The Royal Court's extensive development activity encompasses a diverse range of writers and artists and includes an ongoing programme of writers' attachments, readings, workshops and playwriting groups. Twenty years of pioneering work around the world means the Royal Court has relationships with writers on every continent.

The Royal Court opens its doors to radical thinking and provocative discussion, and to the unheard voices and free thinkers that, through their writing, change our way of seeing.

Within the past sixty years, John Osborne, Arnold Wesker and Howard Brenton have all started their careers at the Court. Many others, including Caryl Churchill, Mark Ravenhill and Sarah Kane have followed.

More recently, the theatre has fostered new writers such as Lucy Kirkwood, Nick Payne, Penelope Skinner and Alistair McDowall and produced many iconic plays from Laura Wade's **Posh** to Jez Butterworth's **Jerusalem** and Martin McDonagh's **Hangmen**.

Royal Court plays from every decade are now performed on stage and taught in classrooms across the globe.

It is because of this commitment to the writer that we believe there is no more important theatre in the world than the Royal Court.

Supported using public funding by
ARTS COUNCIL ENGLAND

ROYAL

IN 2016 THE ROYAL COURT IS 60 YEARS NEW

5 Apr – 7 May
Cyprus Avenue
By David Ireland
Royal Court Theatre and the Abbey Theatre
An Abbey Theatre Commission

17 May – 21 May
Ophelias Zimmer
Directed by Katie Mitchell
Designed by Chloe Lamford
Text by Alice Birch
In association with Schaubühne Berlin

18 May – 18 Jun
Human Animals
By Stef Smith

23 Jun – 9 Jul
Cuttin' It
By Charlene James
A Royal Court/Young Vic co-production
with Birmingham Repertory Theatre,
Sheffield Theatres and The Yard Theatre

1 Jul – 6 Aug
Unreachable
By Anthony Neilson

7 Sep – 15 Oct
Torn
By Nathaniel Martello-White

15 Sep – 22 Oct
Father Comes Home
From The Wars
(Parts 1, 2 & 3)
By Suzan-Lori Parks

Tickets from £10. 020 7565 5000 (no booking fee)
royalcourttheatre.com

 JERWOOD **CHARITABLE** FOUNDATION

Cuttin' It, Human Animals and Torn are all part of the
Royal Court's Jerwood New Playwrights programme,
supported by Jerwood Charitable Foundation

Cyprus Avenue is supported by Cockayne Grants for the Arts, a donor advised fund of London Community Foundation

Innovation partner

Coutts   ARTS COUNCIL ENGLAND
Supported using public funding by
ARTS COUNCIL
ENGLAND

Sloane Square London, SW1W 8AS
🐦 royalcourt 📘 royalcourttheatre
🚇 Sloane Square 🚆 Victoria Station

COURT

ROYAL COURT SUPPORTERS

The Royal Court is a registered charity and not-for-profit company. We need to raise £1.7 million every year in addition to our core grant from the Arts Council and our ticket income to achieve what we do.

We have significant and longstanding relationships with many generous organisations and individuals who provide vital support. Royal Court supporters enable us to remain the writers' theatre, find stories from everywhere and create theatre for everyone.

We can't do it without you.

Coutts supports Innovation at the Royal Court. The Genesis Foundation supports the Royal Court's work with International Playwrights. Bloomberg supports Beyond the Court. Jerwood Charitable Foundation supports emerging writers through the Jerwood New Playwrights series. The Pinter Commission is given annually by his widow, Lady Antonia Fraser, to support a new commission at the Royal Court.

PUBLIC FUNDING

Arts Council England, London
British Council

CHARITABLE DONATIONS

The Austin & Hope Pilkington Trust
Martin Bowley Charitable Trust
The City Bridge Trust
The Clifford Chance Foundation
Cockayne - Grants for the Arts
The Ernest Cook Trust
Cowley Charitable Trust
The Dorset Foundation
The Eranda Foundation
Lady Antonia Fraser for The Pinter Commission
Genesis Foundation
The Golden Bottle Trust

The Haberdashers' Company
Roderick & Elizabeth Jack
Jerwood Charitable Foundation
Kirsh Foundation
The Mackintosh Foundation
Marina Kleinwort Trust
The Andrew Lloyd Webber Foundation
The London Community Foundation
John Lyon's Charity
Clare McIntyre's Bursary
The Andrew W. Mellon Foundation
The Mercers' Company
The Portrack Charitable Trust
The David & Elaine Potter Foundation
The Richard Radcliffe Charitable Trust
Rose Foundation
Royal Victoria Hall Foundation
The Sackler Trust
The Sobell Foundation
John Thaw Foundation
The Vandervell Foundation
Sir Siegmund Warburg's Voluntary Settlement
The Garfield Weston Foundation
The Wolfson Foundation

CORPORATE SPONSORS

AKA
AlixPartners
Aqua Financial Solutions Ltd
Bloomberg
Colbert
Coutts
Edwardian Hotels, London
Fever-Tree
Gedye & Sons

Kudos
MAC
Nyetimber

BUSINESS MEMBERS

Auerbach & Steele Opticians
CNC – Communications & Network Consulting
Cream
Hugo Boss UK
Lansons
Left Bank Pictures
Rockspring Property Investment Managers
Tetragon Financial Group
Vanity Fair

DEVELOPMENT COUNCIL

Majella Altschuler
Piers Butler
Sindy Caplan
Sarah Chappatte
Cas Donald
Celeste Fenichel
Piers Gibson
Emma Marsh
Angelie Moledina
Anatol Orient
Andrew Rodger
Deborah Shaw
Sian Westerman

Innovation partner

Supported using public funding by
ARTS COUNCIL ENGLAND

The Royal Court works with a huge variety of companies ranging from small local businesses to large global firms. The Court has been at the cutting edge of new drama for more than 50 years and, situated in the heart of Chelsea, makes the perfect evening for a night of unique client entertaining.

By becoming a Business Member, your company will be given an allocation of London's hottest tickets with the chance of booking in for sold-out shows, the opportunity to entertain your clients in our stunning Balcony Bar and exclusive access to the creative members of staff and cast members.

To discuss Business Membership at the Royal Court, please contact:
Nadia Vistisen, Development Officer
nadiavistisen@royalcourttheatre.com
020 7565 5030

BECOME A BUSINESS MEMBER

X

for mum.

Characters

Gilda
Mattie
Clark
Cole
Ray

Notes

A question without a question mark denotes a flatness of tone.

– Indicates an interruption of speech or train of thought.

. . . Indicates either a trailing off, a breather, a shift, or a transition.

/ Indicates where the next line of dialogue interrupts or overlaps.

Act One

I.

A small research base on Pluto.

We're in the communal room, which has a table/chairs.

Open exits leading off left and right.

A ladder leading up through an open access hatch above.

A kitchen unit on the back wall.

Above that, a large, circular window that looks out into blackness.

Above that, a large digital clock displaying the time.

It resembles an airport waiting room. Or an expanded train carriage.

Functional and charmless.

It's slightly untidy and cluttered.

It's late.

Gilda *stands,* **Ray** *sits and eats.*

Silence.

Gilda   . . . it's not so long.

Ray   It's long.

Pause.

Ray   It's a long time.

Pause.

Gilda   There was that time – Before, we lost them –

Ray   That's / not –

Gilda   We had nothing from them then –

Ray   They warned us before, we knew that was going to happen, it was *scheduled*.

They were repairing a satellite.

Gilda   Maybe they're doing that now.

Ray   It's completely different.

Gilda   It might just be –

Ray   Two days with prior warning is completely different to three *weeks* radio silence.

. . .

If someone farts out here they want to know about it.

They want a ten-page report on who farted, when they farted, *why* they farted.

You're *Miss* Paperwork for fuck's sake.

That's half the reason they keep us locked to their hours, so they can breathe down our necks easier.

And I've been out here a thousand times and haven't / *once* –

Gilda   Not this far.

Ray   It doesn't matter –

Gilda   *No one's* been out this far –

Ray   Three weeks, no contact, that is a long time. Wherever you are.

. . .

That is a problem.

. . .

It's not something to debate.

Pause.

Gilda *goes to the cupboard and retrieves a box of cereal.*

She eats a handful.

Pause.

Gilda   So then we go through all the systems –

Ray   He says they're fine.

Gilda   So then one of the satellites –

Ray   He says they're fine.

Gilda   If it was fine we'd be talking to them, something is not fine –

Ray   He says everything tech-wise is.

Gilda   There's *something* wrong –

Ray   Of course there's something wrong but it's outside his range of influence.

Gilda   His range of influence?

Ray   Calm down. It's late.

Gilda   You're telling me to panic –

Ray   I'm telling you how it is.

You're a grown woman, calm down.

Beat.

Gilda   I don't like how you talk to me.

Ray   Well.

He takes some pills from a bottle in his pocket.

Gilda   What are those.

Ray   Pills.

Gilda   What pills?

Ray   My pills, it's none of your business what pills, why would I tell you what / pills I take?

Gilda   I'm sorry –

. . .

Sorry.

Pause.

Gilda   So what do we do.

Pause.

Gilda   What can we do?

Ray   Nothing.

Gilda   Noth –

Ray   There's nothing *to* do. We wait.

Gilda   We can't just –

Ray   We're here, they're there.

Gilda   I get that –

Ray   The phone lines are fucked.

Gilda   Yes –

Ray   We can't reach them, they can't reach us.

Gilda   No –

Ray   They're supposed to have picked us up by now –

Gilda   We don't –

Ray   And we've no means of going anywhere ourselves –

Gilda   I know –

Ray   So then what are you asking me for?

What do you think I know that you don't?

You're the genius here, why don't you tell *me* what to do?

Beat.

She blinks.

Oh Jesus Christ.

Gilda   What.

Ray   I can't even have a normal conversation –

You're supposed to be my second in command.

Gilda   I'm *fine* –

Ray   I can't talk to you if you're going to start blubbing
every / time –

Gilda   I'm not 'blubbing'.

Ray   Well it looks like you're doing something.

Gilda   I'm not.

. . .

But if I was,

Which I'm not,

But if I was it would be a perfectly appropriate response to the situation.

Pause.

Ray   They will come and get us.

Maybe they're late, maybe something's wrong, but they'll come.

. . .

And not because of us, but because you don't send billions worth of gear to Pluto then forget about it.

. . .

We've done eighteen months. A few more won't kill us.

Pause.

Gilda   I wasn't crying.

II.

There's a large X smeared across one of the walls in thick, faded brown strokes.

Clark *sits in his boxers. He plays with his balls.*

Mattie *inspects a circuit board.*

A bowl of cereal sits in front of her.

Mattie   How big was it at least?

Clark   I can't remember that far.

Mattie   You just said –

Clark   Not details though. Can't remember details, can I?

It was –

Big. It's a big thing.

She passes the board over.

Clark (*inspecting*)   You've seen em in books.

Mattie   It's obviously not the same. It's a, a *visceral* –

Clark (*passing the board back*)   No.

Mattie   I feel like it's something you'd remember.

Clark   My life's one big blur of sex and adventure, I can't be expected to remember every little thing that ever happened to me.

Mattie   Where was it?

Clark   South America someplace.

Mattie   South America's gone.

Clark   Not then it wasn't, was it. Not when I was six.

Mattie   You were six.

Clark   I was six and it was in this village down there. I was with my uncle.

Mattie   And it was big.

Clark   It was big.

Mattie   And that's it.

Clark   And . . . it was up on this truck.

So it was, you know, even bigger than that. Taller.

Mattie   What about this.

She passes it over again.

Clark (*inspecting*)   . . . What am I looking at.

Mattie   The transistor –

Clark   No, it's fine. It's all fine. I told you.

He tosses it back to her.

Beat.

Mattie   Why was it on a truck?

Clark   Cos. They were taking it away.

Mattie   Who was?

Clark   They were – The blokes – Mexican . . .

Mattie   Mexico's North America.

Clark   Whatever they were. Mexican-looking lads. All stood round the truck with big guns, berets,

Mattie   Why were *you* there?

Clark   I said. I was visiting my uncle. He lived there and he was involved somehow. That's how I got close.

Mattie   You're six and there's guns everywhere –

Clark   My uncle *knows* the dudes with the guns. He's in*volved*.

He goes up to them while they're holding back the crowd –

Mattie   What crowd?

Clark   The crowd, there's a crowd. The whole place – All the little villager guys are trying to get to the truck, and the other guys are all waving guns at them like hallalahhallalahhallalah, Mexican or whatever –

Mattie   Spanish.

Clark   Spanish then –

Mattie   Or not, Portuguese maybe.

Clark   Some fucking thing – Hallalah, hallalah, get back, get back –

And they're all crying and shit,

Mattie   So how did you –

Clark   Because my uncle worked with em, like I said.

He talks to the main army guy in Mexican,

Mattie   Spanish.

Clark   Spanish –

Mattie   Spanish or Portuguese.

Clark   He talks to him like, baddababaddababaddababa, tells them to push the crowd back, let us through, give us some space. And they do, they all get shunted back and pushed away – And my uncle lifts me up and walks over and puts me up on the truck, and I touch it.

Pause.

Mattie   And?

Clark   What.

Mattie   What was it like?

Pause.

Clark   . . . Big.

Mattie   Big.

Clark   They're big. Big fucking tall things.

There's like the main pillar bit, in the middle, then all these webs and lines on top of it, and then the green bits. Leaves.

Mattie   I know what they looked like –

Clark   So there.

Mattie   What was it *like* though. In, *experience* terms.

Pause.

Clark   I dunno.

. . .

It's knobbly.

Main bit's all knobbly. Like rocks.

And the leaves . . .

They're like paper.

Old paper.

Like how paper used to be.

Mattie What did it smell like?

Clark It – I dunno.

You can't remember smells.

I looked at it, I touched it, I got the *gist*.

Then I got lifted back down, they lifted me back down again, and they drove it off.

All the villager guys all running after it shouting.

Chasing it down the road.

Pause.

Mattie That was wasted on you.

Clark Just a tree.

Mattie One of the last *ever*. Do you know how rare that was? To see it? To *touch* it?

Clark And cos I didn't stick my dick in it I'm a philistine.

Mattie You *are* a philistine.

People formed entire *religions* around the last trees.

Clark Yeah, mental people.

Mattie It's a big deal.

Clark Everything used to be a big deal. Coming out here would've been a big deal once.

Mattie It's not the same. My mum used to tell me stories about trees. *Fairy* stories.

Clark So?

Mattie So you touched something considered by an entire generation to be *mythic*. You literally touched the past. That's objectively a big deal.

And you're objectively a moron if you can't understand that.

Clark   I'd say I'm objectively a legend.

Mattie   It's our history.

Clark   It's bullshit. History's bullshit. You're always asking everyone about it and it's *gone*. It doesn't exist. I don't waste my time thinking about shit that doesn't exist.

Mattie   So you never think about the past then.

Clark   No.

Mattie   Not ever.

Clark   No. That's why I'm way cooler than you.

Mattie   What about the future.

Clark   No. Same thing. Doesn't exist. Can't see it. Touch it. There's just this second, right now, as I'm saying it it's dying, it's gone. There it goes.

Pimps like me live in the present.

Cole *comes in to make his lunch.*

Clark   You wanna talk to Cole about what a waste of fucking time worrying about tomorrow is.

Cole –

Cole tell us about your bomb shelter again.

Cole   I'm busy.

Clark   Just tell us though. Cole. Cole.

Mattie   / I don't care –

Clark   Tell us. Cole.

Mattie *gets up and leaves, taking her cereal with her.*

Enter **Gilda**.

Clark   Cole.

Cole.

Gilda   Clark –

Clark   Cole tell Gilda about your bomb shelter.

Cole   / I'm busy.

Gilda   I don't care –

Clark   Just tell us. Cole. Cole.

Tell us. Cole –

Cole   I have a bomb shelter.

Clark   Yeah, but –

Cole   That's the story.

Clark   Tell us about what it's all got though.

Gilda   / I don't –

Cole   Air filtration, water purifiers,

Clark   All fucking kitted out, yeah –

Gilda   / I've heard all this –

Cole   It's a bomb shelter.

Clark   And he got it cos he thought we were gonna get done –

Cole   It seemed a strong possibility at the time.

Clark   And how much was it?

Cole   I already told you –

Clark   Tell me again though –

Gilda   Clark –

Cole   I had to remortgage my apartment.

Clark   WHAT A FUCKING RETARD!

He laughs hysterically.

Gilda   Clark –

Clark   His whole apartment!

Cole   It was an investment.

Gilda   Clark, can you –

Clark   Why would you wanna stay around if everything's nuked to fuck anyway?

Gilda   *Clark.*

Clark   What?

Pause.

Gilda   I asked you to clean that wall.

Clark   What.

Gilda   The wall. I asked you –

I asked you to clean it weeks ago –

Clark   Days ago.

Gilda   *Weeks* ago, I told you, I asked you to do it *weeks* ago –

Clark   Nah it was like yesterday.

Gilda   It doesn't matter when,

Clark   Cole wasn't it just yesterday?

Gilda   / It doesn't matter when it was –

Cole   I don't –

Clark   We're still running on Earth hours aren't we?

Gilda   Don't start –

Clark   *Universal* Time. Less you decided to switch us to a hundred and fifty-three hour days without letting us know?

Gilda   All I've asked you to do –

Clark   I don't think I'm allowed to.

Gilda   Clark –

Clark   My contract expired.

. . .

Right?

All our contracts expired. *Months* ago.

When they were meant to pick us up.

Cole *leaves with his lunch.*

Gilda   The situation means –

Clark   Supposed to be home by now.

I'm not insured.

I can't work if I'm not insured.

Gilda   Everyone has to do their bit –

Clark   That's not *my* bit. Cleaning isn't even *in* my contract.

I'm in a union –

Gilda   We're all in a union –

Clark   I can't be expected to do unpaid work –

Off-world unpaid work, which is often hazardous –

Gilda   It's cleaning a wall.

Clark   What if I go to do it and I slip and I fall down –

Gilda   You're –

Clark   Then I'm not just stranded on a cold dark rock in space, I'm stranded on a cold dark rock in space with a broken leg, or arm, or *spine*, with only very limited medical facilities –

Gilda   Can you listen to me?

Clark   You don't wanna get back to Earth and find a lawsuit waiting for you, that'd take the shine off the rescue, don't you think?

Gilda   Can you *listen* to me for a second please?

Pause.

Gilda   I only asked you –

Clark   Why am I cleaning it off? You think I *want* to clean it off?

Gilda   I'm just trying to –

Clark   I'm not joking about the union –

Gilda   Well *call them then*!

Pause.

Gilda   Call them.

But to do that you'd have to actually do your *job* first and fix our communications –

Clark   How many times do you want me to fucking tell you?

Comms are fine. They're *fine*.

Gilda Clearly they're not Clark, because if they were, we wouldn't still *be* here –

Clark I don't come into your little lab and start fucking around with your rocks, but you get to come and knock the dick out of *my* mouth whenever you want, and tell me what a shit job I'm doing when you don't know anything about it. *Anything*.

You think it's *my* fault we're still here.

You think it's *my* fault they haven't come to take us home –

Gilda That's not what I'm / saying –

Clark Every single transmission we've made has been marked as received.

. . .

Okay?

. . .

Do you get what that means?

. . .

Our computer. Their computers. Everything works.

Everything we send is getting to Earth.

Every broadcast. Video, audio, text. Received. Tick.

Everything's getting there.

Fine.

But no one's sending anything back.

. . .

No one's on *their* end of the phone.

. . .

Okay?

. . .

I can't make someone who's not *there* answer our
transmissions.

Pause.

Gilda   You're being ridiculous.

Clark   Am I.

Gilda   That's a completely – Ridiculous thing to assume –

Clark   What is.

Gilda   That they're – That everyone's just –

. . .

Pause.

Gilda   We're all a bit –

Fraught.

From, from being out here so long,

not getting picked up when we're supposed to get picked
up,

not having any contact for a few months –

Clark   Six mon / ths.

Gilda   *Nearly* six months.

Clark   It's six –

Gilda   Whatever it is, however long –

The last contact we had from them was delaying our
return –

Clark   By a few days –

Gilda   So then maybe it got delayed more, there's a bigger delay and they can't get through to, to tell us when they're actually coming,

Clark   They can get through fine.

Gilda   We're billions of miles from Earth –

Clark   So?

Gilda   So *what's* more likely?

. . .

Sta*tistically*.

. . .

That the whole programme just decided to forget about us and leave us out here?

Or that in the space of six months the entire human race has dropped down dead?

. . .

. . .

Or is it possible, somewhere,

maybe,

in the *billions* of miles between here and there,

there's just maybe something *wrong*?

. . .

What do you think?

Mattie *has come back, listening in the doorway, unnoticed.*

Pause.

Clark   Even if I did find something wrong,

I can't *do* anything with that information.

We can't go anywhere –

We can't get off the ground –

Gilda   So what do you want me to say?

. . .

Tell me what I should say to you.

Pause.

Clark *picks up the circuit board.*

Pause.

Gilda   Thank you.

. . .

And will you –

Clark   I'll *clean* it.

Gilda   Good. Thank you.

. . .

And maybe you could start wearing clothes again.

She leaves.

Pause.

Clark *grumbles something.*

Mattie   What?

Beat.

Clark   I said it won't make any difference.

In the transition, **Mattie** *leaves.*

Clark *puts some clothes on and cleans the X from the wall.*

It takes as long as it takes.

III.

Late.

Clark *and* **Ray**.

Ray   Luscinia megarhynchos.

Clark   Luscina –

Ray   Luscinia.

Clark   Luscinia –

Ray   Luscinia megarhynchos.

Clark   Luscinia mega –

Ray   Megarhynchos.

Clark   Luscinia megarhynchos.

Ray   Nightingale.

Ray *blows a bird whistle.*

Clark   That's nice. That's a nice one.

Ray   Phylloscopus trochilos.

Clark   Filla – I won't even – That's all yours, that one.

Ray   Willow Warbler.

He blows a bird whistle.

Clark   That's nice too.

Ray   Regulus Regulus.

Clark   Regulus Regulus. That's easier.

Ray   Regulus Regulus, Goldcrest.

He blows a bird whistle.

Clark   Regulus Regulus.

. . .

I like the first one best.

Ray   Me too.

Clark   Luscinia –

Ray   Luscinia megarhynchos.

Clark   Nightingale. You can just say nightingale.

Ray   That's not the point though, is it.

He starts putting them away.

Clark   You blow em a lot.

Ray   Course I do.

Clark   A lot though, Ray. Arguably too much.

Ray   Do you know why?

Clark   Cos it's nice.

Ray   Course it's nice, goes without saying it's nice.

I wouldn't do it that much if it was just *nice*.

Clark   It's really nice.

Ray   I do it so I don't forget.

To *remember*.

Clark   Right.

Ray   Out here.

Clark   Yeah.

Ray   No internet, no . . .

Clark   You can't just listen to bird sounds.

Ray   These are all I have.

And I have to blow em a certain way –

Clark   To make the right sound.

Ray   So if I don't blow em every day then they start to not sound right.

Then after a while I forget what they ever sounded like.

Then they're gone.

. . .

When you're away it's very easy to start forgetting.

Once you've detached yourself.

Clark   But when you got back you could –

Ray   Even then, even when I get back to Earth, there's only *recordings*.

And that's just another form of memory, cept it's a computer remembering instead of you.

. . .

I try very hard to hold onto birds in particular.

He blows a whistle.

Ray   I'm just about old enough to remember the day they all fell out the trees.

. . .

My father comes in my room with a brush and says come help.

I follow him outside and they're all lying in the street.

Like stones wrapped in paper.

. . .

First the trees stopped singing. Then they stopped breathing.

The colour left.

Then the light.

Then nothing.

. . .

Beat.

Clark   Fucking hell Ray.

Ray   What.

Clark   You're bringing me down.

Ray   Well, you don't know. You've no memory of what it was like.

I'm the last generation that lived amongst the living.

Clark   Let's play a game or something, Jesus.

He sets up Guess Who.

Ray   Not this, let's play chess.

Clark   You always beat me.

Ray   That's why I like it.

Clark   We're playing Guess Who. Pick a guy.

They look at the cards.

And don't just pick Bernard again, you always use him.

They pick cards.

Ray   You're not interested in the past.

Clark   Pimps live in the present, Ray.

Are you a guy or a girl?

Ray   What? Oh. I'm a – Female.

Clark *flicks panels down.*

Ray   They all think I'm an old fart too.

Clark   I don't think you're an old fart Ray.

I just think you're depressing as fuck.

Ray   That's what they all think.

Clark   Who?

Ray   On Earth. The pricks who write the cheques. Why do you think they sent me out here, with you lot? To a planet that's not a planet.

Clark   I think it's alright.

Ray   You've never been to Mars. Titan. Real planets.

Clark   Titan's not a planet mate.

Ray   More than this. More than rocks and ice and darkness.

Clark   They reckon if we'd come here before the sun started fannying out it would've been almost daylight sometimes.

Ray   Hmph.

Clark   Ask me something.

Ray   Are you male.

Clark   Yes.

Ray *flicks panels down.*

Ray   It's the biggest insult they could manage.

Making me ferry a bunch of green scientists out here then sit around waiting for someone half my age to come collect me.

We used to fly *back* from places too, not just ship these flat packs out.

Clark   Someone's gotta set up base.

Do you have short hair.

Ray   No.

Clark *flicks panels down.*

Ray   There's a reason no one's been here before, it's that no one in their right mind would ever *want* to come here.

They know there's nothing useful here.

It's a financial work-around. It's a tax write-off.

This is where they send the new, the underqualified, the old.

And most of all the British. Mars is full of blonde Americans.

It's like they're building the master race out there.

He takes his pills.

Clark   They should use you in the recruitment adverts Ray.

Ray   Why did you want to do it?

Clark   Do what?

Ray   Come out here.

Clark   I dunno . . .

Ray   Are you wearing a hat?

Clark   Wh – No.

Ray *flips panels down.*

Ray   There are reasons a person signs up to work this far from home.

Clark   Gilda says she wanted to work off-world since she was a kid.

Ray   Well she's a hopeless case. What about you. Why did *you* want to come out here.

Clark   . . . Tax free's pretty good.

Ray   It's a perk.

Clark   You get to keep all your money.

Ray   There are easier ways to avoid tax.

Clark   I liked the idea. Being an astronaut.

Ray   Yes.

Clark   I liked all the old films.

Ray   A symbol.

Clark   Yeah –

Ray   The last cowboys.

Clark   And it's alright out here. I mean, the food's pretty bad –

Ray   It's the same.

Clark   Nah –

Ray   It's just the same back there.

Clark   A burger though –

Ray   I remember when meat came from animals. Not a production line of petri dishes.

Clark   It tastes the same.

Ray   How would you know?

Clark   They say –

Ray   Course *they* say, what are they likely to say it tastes like shit?

Clark   Yeah, but –

Ray   Who's going to prove them wrong, there's nothing left to kill to prove them wrong. Everything's dead.

Clark   Tastes pretty good to me.

Ray   Nothing tastes better than something that used to run around and have thoughts.

My mouth moistens up just thinking about it, and the last time I ate real meat I was five years old.

Just now, just thinking about it now.

It's moist city in here.

Clark   That's great Ray.

Ray   I don't even think about sex these days. Just food. *Real* food.

Clark *shakes his head.*

Ray   You don't get that from the crap they feed us now.

It's like swallowing cardboard.

Clark   It's not that bad.

Ray   If those are your only reasons for being here . . .

Clark   No, I like, I like all of it.

I get the annoying bits.

Staring at the same faces every day. No offence.

Recycled air, recycled water. Breathing each others' farts, drinking each others' piss.

And I've never gotten used to the bogs.

. . .

But I still like putting my suit on, when I'm checking the lines or whatever.

Going out on the surface.

Looking up at the moon, the stars.

Mist.

Everything.

It's class.

Ray   Ever see anything else out there?

Beat.

Clark   Like what?

Pause.

Clark   Like –

Like what?

Pause.

Clark What else would I see out there?

Ray Are we playing this stupid game or what.

Pause.

Clark Uh – Do you have white hair.

Ray Yes.

Clark *flips panels down.*

Pause.

Ray Do you want to hear my secret plan?

Clark Are you Susan.

Ray Yes, well done, full marks. Do you want to hear.

Clark It's late, Ray.

Ray Late by whose watch? It's late in London but maybe it's lunchtime on Pluto.

Clark I don't live on Plutonian time.

Ray Do you want to hear.

Pause.

Clark What's your secret plan.

Pause.

Ray One of these runs, one time, maybe even this one, but one of them, wherever they send me, I'm not going back.

Pause.

Clark   What – To Earth?

Ray   Course to Earth, where else?

Clark   You'd stay here.

Ray   Here, there, wherever. One of these bases. They've got enough juice in these things for decades. Multiple missions. Indefinite timescale.

I could last it out comfortably.

Clark   Why would you *want* to?

Ray   Why would I want to go back? What have I got back there?

Two ex-wives and a bedsit full of old photographs.

That's not living.

Clark   And out here is?

Ray   There's nothing left back there. Trees. Birds. Animals. Countries gone.

Everyone crammed too close together on what's left of the land.

It's a shadow.

And they want to retire me. Trap me there.

Well fuck them.

I'll stay out here and go on my own terms.

Clark   Ray, that's – Not a good idea.

Ray   I'm not going to sputter out in my apartment where no one finds me.

Wait for the worms to eat me away. Stop being able to breathe through the smog.

Die in some riot I didn't even know was happening.

. . .

Everything that place was left a long time ago.

And I'd rather be dead a few billion miles away than alive in the wreckage.

IV.

Late.

Gilda *is alone.*

She eats from a box of cereal and looks out the window.

Her laptop's open on the table.

She walks the room, eating.

Mutters to herself.

There's a noise from above.

She stops.

Listens.

Someone's moving around up there.

We listen for a while.

Mattie *appears in the doorway, unnoticed.*

The sounds have stopped.

Gilda *squints to hear –*

Mattie   What / are you doing?

Gilda   Ah! Jesus –

You –

Made me jump.

Mattie *turns the lights on.*

Mattie   Why are you in the dark?

Gilda   Not completely dark –

Mattie   What were you doing, just then?

Gilda   I couldn't –

. . .

I thought you were up there, and I –

Mattie   I'm down here.

Gilda   I thought I heard someone.

Mattie   No one goes up there cept me.

Gilda   I know –

Mattie   You can't stand up in there.

Gilda   I just thought I heard someone.

. . .

Obviously I didn't.

Pause.

Mattie *goes to the ladder.*

Gilda   Don't –

Mattie   Why?

Gilda   It's – Stupid.

Mattie *goes up the ladder.*

Pause.

Mattie (*from above*)   Oh my god . . .

Gilda   What?

Mattie (*from above*)   There's . . . Nothing up here.

Gilda   Alright.

Mattie *comes back down.*

Gilda   Don't need / to . . .

Mattie   Everything that keeps us alive is up there, you probably heard the girls talking.

Gilda   The girls?

Mattie   The girls are what I call the oxygen and water systems.

Gilda   Oh.

. . .

That's nice.

Mattie   Are you eating cereal?

Gilda   No, yes, just, Krispy Wows.

Mattie   You eat them dry like that?

Gilda   A bit. Sometimes.

Pause.

They stand there.

Mattie Well. Night.

She goes to leave.

Gilda Oh, Mattie –

I'd like to – To run tests on the, uh, 'girls' tomorrow. If that's okay.

Mattie I run tests every day.

Gilda I know –

Mattie That's my job.

Gilda I know, I'd just like to, watch.

If that's okay.

Mattie (*shrugs*) Whatever yanks your crank.

She goes to leave again.

Gilda I'd like to be more involved.

Mattie Okay.

Gilda I think it'd be useful.

Mattie You're the chief, Chief.

She goes to leave again.

Gilda Oh, sorry, Mattie?

I –

. . .

Why did you let me say Ray's name wrong?

. . .

Mattie His –

Gilda His surname.

. . .

. . .

I was saying it wrong. The whole time.

. . .

No one ever told me.

Pause.

Gilda And then at his, the funeral, the service thing we did, you were *laughing* –

Mattie It's not a big –

Gilda At his *funeral*.

Pause.

Mattie He thought it was funny. To not correct you.
It wasn't really about *you*, it was just . . .

Beat.

Gilda It's mean.

Mattie Yeah.

Gilda   It's a mean thing to do to someone.

Mattie   It is, yeah.

Gilda   He might've liked me a bit more if I hadn't said his name wrong the entire time. *Years*.

Sih-bow-ski –

Mattie   Suh-*botch*-ki –

Gilda   I know *now* –

Mattie *nods*.

Gilda   You told me after we'd wheeled him in the *freezer*.

Pause.

Did I do something to you at some point?

Mattie   No –

Gilda   Something I did that I didn't realise –

Mattie   You didn't do anything –

Gilda   Because I didn't *want* to be Captain –

Mattie   I know –

Gilda   And I'm well aware I'm terrible at it but I *have* to do it.

Mattie   / You're n –

Gilda   And you get to take the piss and not listen and have fun – don't you think *I'd* like to do that too?

Mattie   / I –

Gilda   You just leave me with Cole who is *no one* to talk to, *I* don't like him either but if I didn't talk to him I wouldn't talk to *anyone* –

And how am I supposed to be in charge if you both think I'm this total dickhead

Mattie   / I don't –

Gilda   who can't do anything right and doesn't get the jokes and makes you do work you don't want to do –

Well fuck me for trying to get us home, for trying to keep us together after everything that happened,

And –

And I can't *do* this, I can't *be* in charge or Acting Captain or whatever the paperwork says I have to be – I'm just / supposed to be studying *rocks*, I can't, I can't –

Mattie   Please don't – Gilda –

Gilda.

. . .

. . .

I'm sorry.

. . .

. . .

Okay?

. . .

. . .

. . .

Are you crying?

Gilda   No –

Mattie   You're breathing weird –

Gilda   I'm – Fine.

Pause.

Mattie   . . . Is it cos you thought you heard a ghost?

Gilda   I didn't –

Mattie   Okay –

Gilda   I don't think I heard a ghost. It was just what you said.

Mattie   Right. The girls.

Gilda   The girls.

Mattie   Right.

Pause.

Gilda *gradually gets herself together.*

Gilda   That was unbelievably pathetic.

Mattie   No . . .

Gilda   Really, completely, pathetic.

Mattie   No, it was –

. . .

Fine.

. . .

. . .

Pause.

Mattie   I don't think you're a dickhead.

. . .

If you're . . .

. . .

And,

I don't think it matters if you're not good at being in charge.

Not that you're not good, I mean –

The wall's clean now, right?

You got that done.

Gilda   You don't need to try and cheer me up.

Mattie   I'm not – I'm just saying I don't think it's – I don't think it matters.

. . .

Because what even is there to be in charge *of* right now?

I mean –

We're just *waiting*. Waiting for someone to pick up the phone. Or come get us.

. . .

Or we're just waiting to die.

Gilda   Don't say that.

Mattie   Well it's true.

And there's nothing you can do about that.

We've got more than enough food. Water won't run out.

And the base is designed to last for *decades*, it'll still be breathing *way* after we've stopped. Its *job* is to live forever.

. . .

And that's the really scary thought.

. . .

I used to lie awake worrying about the windows cracking, now I worry about them *not* ever cracking.

. . .

You know?

. . .

Cos I would definitely punch my card if I thought I was just gonna be sat here.

Forever.

Staring at the walls.

Sat here till I lose every last one of my marbles and start eating my own shit without noticing the smell.

. . .

Gilda   . . .

I said you didn't have to try and cheer me up.

Mattie   I'm just saying I hope I go first.

Beat.

Gilda   . . . Next.

. . .

You hope you go next.

Pause.

Mattie   Right.

. . .

Yeah.

Pause.

Gilda *chews her hair.*

Mattie   What are you doing?

Gilda   Oh – (*Stopping.*)

Mattie   Do you do that a lot?

Gilda   Not –

Really.

Mattie   You were doing it just then.

Gilda   It's just when I'm anxious.

Mattie   I make you anxious?

Gilda   Everything makes me anxious. It's not you specifically.

Mattie   So you're always doing it.

Gilda   Not *always*.

Mattie   Why don't you just masturbate like everyone else?

Gilda   I don't – Does that help?

Mattie   Course it does. It's your release valve.

And what else are we meant to do all day anyway?

Gilda   I mean – Work –

Mattie   I'm on my DJ decks like three times a day.

Gilda   Three *times*?

Mattie   At least. I call it Nasturbating. Cos of Nasa.

Gilda   We're not with Nasa.

Mattie   I know, but, you know.

What about you?

Gilda   I'm not –

Mattie   Come on. We're talking.

Gilda   I don't usually talk about –

Mattie   Come *on* . . .

Beat.

Gilda   I don't do a lot of DJ sets.

Mattie   What, ever?

Gilda   R –

Rarely.

Mattie   You'd definitely feel way better about everything if you did.

Gilda   I doubt it.

Mattie   It's a good way of giving the day structure, too.

I know we're locked to Earth hours but it barely means anything when it's always dark, so if I rub one out morning noon and night it gives everything a bit more shape.

And it keeps me cool generally.

Gilda   I just eat.

Mattie   Yeah.

Gilda   Or chew –

She chews her hair.

Mattie   Well you definitely shouldn't do that.

Gilda   I know.

Mattie   Mostly because it makes you look touched but also because I read about this girl who died once and they didn't know why? So they opened her up and all her internal organs were like, *garrotted* with hair.

Gilda   Right –

Mattie   Because she chewed her hair.

Gilda   Yeah, I mean, that's probably a myth.

Mattie   I read it.

Gilda   I'm not *swallowing* it –

Mattie   No, but –

Gilda   And if I did it'd go to my stomach, not my kidneys or my pancreas or wherever else.

Mattie   Well maybe it's not a hundred per cent but the point remains it's not a good habit to have.

You're anxious though, you get anxious?

Gilda   When I start thinking about never getting home.

Mattie   Right, yeah, course. Sorry.

. . .

Who's waiting for you. Back there.

Gilda   My –

. . .

Beat.

She frowns.

Mattie   What?

Gilda   Nothing, I –

. . .

I was about to say my mother.

Mattie   Your mum's waiting for you?

Gilda   No, she's –

Died.

Just before we left.

. . .

I don't know why I . . .

. . .

Beat.

Mattie   Was she old?

Gilda   Hm?

Mattie   Your mum.

Gilda   She was –

Quite old. Not so old.

She could've –

She was sick.

. . .

She got very . . .

Jumbled.

. . .

Mattie   I'm sorry.

Gilda   No, it's –

It's a long time ago now I guess.

. . .

Pause.

Mattie   What are you listening to?

Gilda   Oh – Nothing –

Mattie   Come on, you never tell anyone what you're into.

Gilda   It's nothing – I mean –

I don't sleep much at the moment, so it's just something to, um, relax to.

Mattie   So what is it?

Gilda   It's just –

. . .

With everything whirring away it never gets properly quiet in here, so I like to take a recorder out on surface walks and I, I'll record, you know, outside.

The nothing out there.

Beat.

Mattie   You're listening to nothing.

Gilda   And I sit here with the lights off and look out the window and sort of, zone out a bit.

Mattie   Like meditation.

Gilda   I guess. Almost. Kind of.

Mattie   You can't just listen to a blank audio file?

Gilda   It's different. It has a . . .

An organic quality. The type of silence I get.

It – Breathes.

Mattie   It doesn't.

Gilda   No, I know, but – It's – Real. Real . . . nothingness.

Beat.

Mattie   I only asked to change the subject but this is more depressing.

Gilda (*laughs*)   It's not, I like it.

It's nice.

Pause.

Mattie   Do you want to hear a story about Ray?

Gilda   About Ray?

Mattie   It's kind of amazing.

Gilda   It's not another attempt to cheer me up.

Mattie   No –

Gilda   I don't want to hear some . . . I don't want to make fun –

Mattie   It's not –

Gilda   Some mean story about –

Mattie   It's not, I promise.

Pause.

Mattie   Okay?

Gilda   Okay.

Mattie   Okay –

So –

This is,

I don't know,

a while ago.

Maybe a few weeks before he died.

And I'm in here and he's in here and it's late, he always liked to sit up late.

I don't think he slept much.

And he was in a weird mood, I don't know,

Maybe he'd been drinking but he didn't *seem* –

He just seemed tired. Stressed, or whatever.

And we talk for a bit even though he's kind of distracted and cagey and just being generally –

Weird.

And that was one of the days I'd been outside to check all the lines, and he started asking me, Did I see anything out there, Did I see anything out there.

And I thought –

I was saying –

In the sky? The mist? Shooting stars?

And he says no, Did I *see* anything.

Gilda   See what?

Mattie   This is what I'm asking, I'm like, Like what? What else would I see out there?

And he says 'I saw something'.

. . .

And I say what, because he barely even went outside, what
could he see just sitting here, but he says –

'I saw a girl.'

. . .

. . .

He says 'I saw a girl. At the window.'

. . .

. . .

So I thought he was joking, or, I mean, sometimes he said
pretty weird things,

so I didn't –

But he's just staring at me, completely like –

Like slate.

. . .

. . .

He says I saw a little girl.

Maybe four or five. Small.

Looking in at him. Watching.

. . .

. . .

And after a while she just walks away, out of sight.

And he goes looking out all the windows all over trying to, to
see where she went to, but he can't see her.

She's gone.

. . .

. . .

. . .

Isn't that amazing?

Gilda   A girl –

Mattie   Just stood outside the window. Watching him.

Pause.

Gilda   But –

Mattie   I mean, obviously it's impossible but that's not the point.

The point is he really *believed* he saw it.

I believed, that he believed.

And after that, for the last month he was –

Well.

. . .

And now he's gone.

Pause.

Mattie   I just thought, since you thought *you* heard something –

Gilda   I didn't –

Mattie   I know, but –

You know.

Pause.

Gilda   That's awful.

Mattie   I know.

Gilda   It's –

Mattie   I know.

Pause.

Gilda   Poor Ray.

Mattie   Poor Ray.

Pause.

Mattie   Oh man,

I even missed the –

He said she had a,

The girl?

She had a kind of a –

The mouth.

It was all fucked up.

Beat.

Gilda   What do you mean.

Mattie   Instead of a mouth she had this –

Scar.

A big scar or a scab or something.

Gilda   Like what?

Mattie   Like this –

She slowly draws an X across her mouth with her finger.

Pause.

He kept saying – What happens when she gets inside?
What happens when she gets in here?

. . .

. . .

'What happens when she gets inside?'

Pause.

Mattie   Can I hear some of your silence?
Gilda   Oh –

Mattie *yanks the headphones out the laptop.*

Gilda   It won't really work out the speakers –

Mattie *hits play.*

All the sound is sucked out of the room.

It's as if the whole scene is plunged under water.

They stand in the total silence, feeling it move around them.

Mattie   It's nice . . .

Pause.

A crackle.

A voice starts to pull out of the laptop.

Neither of them seem to hear it as it dribbles out the speakers,

Then fills the theatre.

Voice   Hellooooo . . .
. . .
Hello!

Laughter.

The voice of a very young girl.

Ah-Boo!
Ah-Boo!
Boo!
BOO!
. . .
onetwothreefourfivesixseveneightblargleblargleblurrblurr

blrrfff –

Laughter.

You can make your, in here, you can take it in here, and, and
you can take it and you can, you can put it back in for later.
Put it back in for later and make it here so you can have it for
later with me.

The lights drop leaving us alone with the voice.

It whispers –

And it's all –

All the colours.

To put it back to make it before and you can have it for later.

For if you,

For when you *need* them.

So you can always have them . . .

. . .

Laughter.

V.

Late.

Cole *is working at the table with paper and pencil.*

Clark *is semi-clothed, tossing a ball around.*

He starts hurling the ball against walls and catching it.

He hums and sings tunelessly. Big sighs and annoying noises.

This goes on for a while.

Cole *is visibly irritated.*

Eventually **Clark***'s ball crashes into the kitchen unit, clattering plates everywhere.*

Cole   Can you do that somewhere else.

Clark   I'm *bored* man. So *bored*.

Cole   Be bored somewhere else.

Clark   Usually when I'm bored I'll have a wank but I've used up all my porn.

He bounces the ball again.

I never thought that'd happen. I brought *so* much.

But we've been here so long now.

. . .

I wish I'd brought more normal films to be honest.

. . .

What films have you got?

. . .

Can I copy some of your films?

. . .

Cole.

. . .

Cole.

. . .

Cole.

. . .

Cole –

Cole   I don't have any.

Clark   What?

Cole   I don't like films.

Beat.

Clark   What do you mean? Who doesn't like *films*?

Cole   I don't like anything fictional.

Clark   Why?

Cole   Because it's made up. I don't like things that aren't real.

Pause.

Clark   You're a fucking weirdo man. That is such a weird thing to say.

What kind of reason is that?

What are you doing anyway?

He picks up some of **Cole**'s *papers.*

Cole   Don't touch that –

Clark   Maths? You do know maths is for benders, yeah?

Cole   Put it down.

Clark   This is what you do instead of watching films. Recreational maths.

He goes back to throwing his ball.

Cole   I'm trying to work –

Clark   Do you think I'm mean to Gilda?

Cole   I don't know –

Clark   I don't mean to be –

Like I mean I do,

But it gets out of hand.

And I like her too, I think she's alright.

She just gets well stressed. About us being stuck here so long.

And I am too you know, I just don't see what we can do about it.

So I don't worry about it.

. . .

But you never seem bothered about anything.

You're always just the same.

But I bet it's hardest for you, actually.

Cole   Why.

Clark   Cos you've got a kid.

Cole   Oh. Yes.

Clark   I don't think I'd even *come* out here if I had a kid.
If I had a kid I'd want to be there. For *everything*.

. . .

Do you miss him loads?

. . .

Do you reckon he's in your bomb shelter now?

. . .

How old is he?

. . .

Cole.

. . .

Cole.

. . .

Cole –

Cole   What can I say that'll make you go somewhere else.

Clark   Why can't you go somewhere else?

Cole   I – Need something in here.

Clark   You need a calculator mate, your maths is gash.

Beat.

Clark   Do you miss Ray?

Cole   What do you mean.

Clark I think about him a lot. I sometimes –

Cole What do you mean about my maths.

Beat.

Clark It's ballbags. It's wrong.

Cole How would you know.

Clark Because I'm a Mathematician and Computer Scientist, dickhead.

Fuck's sake, everyone thinks I'm a total retard round here –

Cole You only saw it for a second.

Clark Long enough to smell the shit in your equations.

Do you want me to write you an algorithm?

Beat.

Cole What for?

Clark (*makes a face*) Ummnnh! To help solve whatever you're trying to solve quicker.

Beat.

Cole How long will that take.

Clark Depends.

Cole On what.

Clark On whether I want to do it or not.

Beat.

Cole   I can do it myself.

Clark   Alright then.

He throws his ball at the walls again.

Pause.

Cole   What do you – What do you want.

Clark   For what.

Cole   For the algorithm.

Clark   I don't want anything mate. Just respect. Brotherhood.

And that laser pointer keyring you have, I want that.

Cole   My keyring.

Clark   It's a big job, writing an algorithm.

Beat.

Cole *sighs and takes his keys out.*

He works the laser pointer off the ring and passes it to **Clark**.

Clark   Nice.

Cole   Now – Stop that –

Clark *is shining it in* **Cole**'s *face.*

Cole   Stop it. Write it for me.

Clark   What's it for.

Cole   I gave you the keyring –

Clark   I can't write it without details, can I?

What's it for, what are we looking for?

The un*known*.

What's X?

Pause.

What?

Cole   I can give you the figures, but –

Clark   S'alright, not that bothered. This got old anyway –

He tosses the keyring and goes to leave.

Cole   Time. X is time.

Pause.

Clark   Time.

Cole *nods*.

Clark   You want an algorithm for time.

Pause.

There's a clock right there mate.

You're taking the long way round.

And we're wearing watches –

Cole   Watch it. Watch.

They watch the clock.

Time passes.

Clark   What are you –
Cole   Watch.

Pause.

The display stutters, faults,

then snaps backwards one hour and forty-three minutes.

Pause.

Clark   What – What was that.

Pause.

It's broke. Why didn't you tell me, now I have to –
Cole   You can't fix it.
Clark (*checking watch*)   What time do you –
Cole   You can't fix it.
. . .
The watches are the same. The computers.

They're all the same.

. . .

Everything's linked to Earth through the main clock.

And the main clock's wrong.

Pause.

Clark   How long's it been like that?

Cole   I don't know.

Clark   But you're –

Cole   How could I tell?

. . .

It goes back every night. Multiple times.

Sometimes in the day too, but not as often.

. . .

And that's what we're assuming's day and night.

Clark   Every day.

Cole   Sometimes minutes, sometimes hours. Sometimes it just slows down.

I saw it go back a week once.

Monday to Monday.

I thought someone'd notice that one but I suppose we're all trying not to think about time too much.

. . .

It's been doing it more recently. That's why we've been sleeping so badly.

Pause.

Clark   We don't know what time it is.

Cole   No.

Clark   Or what day.

Cole   No.

Pause.

Clark   So we don't know long we've been here.

Cole   No.

Clark   We think it's nearly three years –

Cole   It's more. Maybe lots more.

We had a day 'last week' that lasted at least fifty hours.

You had a lot of naps.

Pause.

Clark   But we're – No – It's not –

Cole   Will you do the algorithm now.

Clark   Why didn't we notice?

Cole   A day here is six and a half Earth days.

And the sun's barely visible and we're always inside.

It's one long night.

That's why they fixed everything to Universal Time on Earth.

It's supposed to be more reliable.

Clark   But it's *fucked*.

Cole   Yes.

The computers don't log Plutonian time either.

Which is why I need the algorithm.

Clark   That wouldn't –

If it's that random there's no way you could ever –

Cole   I know. It's more of a hobby.

Beat.

Clark   What about – What did Gilda say?

Cole   What.

Clark   When you told her.

Cole   I didn't tell her.

Clark   Why?

Cole   Why would I.

Clark   She's in charge –

Cole   She can't do anything. No one can do anything.

The fault's somewhere between here and Earth.

Clark   That's not the point –

Cole   What would it achieve.

Clark   If you'd told someone as soon as you'd –

Cole   I don't know how long it was doing this before I noticed.

Or even how long since I noticed.

It would have made no difference.

Clark   You told me.

Cole   You made me tell you.

Clark   So you've just been watching us like lab rats?

Cole   I didn't think you'd want to know.

Do you feel better knowing.

Pause.

Clark   No.

Pause.

This is why a lot of the systems keep glitching.

Cole   Everything's centralised.

Beat.

Clark   Well what can we – There's gotta be –

He rifles through **Cole***'s notes and finds an analogue watch.*

Cole   It's broken. I think he wore it just because.

Clark   He –

. . .

How did you get this?

. . .

Did you take this off his body?

Pause.

Cole   I needed –

Clark   The fuck is *wrong* with you?!

Cole   It wasn't –

Clark   You took this off his *wrist* –

Cole   It was *important*. There's no time to be sentimental when we're –

Clark   He was our friend –

Cole   He wasn't my friend.

Clark   Well he was still a human being for *fuck's* sake.

. . .

He pockets the watch.

Pause.

Cole   There's no point getting upset.

. . .

Can't get it back now.

Clark *looks up at the clock.*

Pause.

I don't know how old I am.

The clock faults again –

VI.

Late.

The table is strewn with photographs.

Ray *sits clutching a bloody cloth to his arm.*

Gilda *looks on.*

Pause.

Ray   Even if we were in contact with them, what would they do.

Pause.

Gilda   That's not the point.

Ray   I doubt they'd care enough to spend a few million sending a taxi home for me.

Gilda   Ray –

Ray   They'd just tell you to restrain me. Keep me tied up for months till whichever young prick they send shows up. If he does ever show up.

Gilda   You're not allowed to downplay this.

Pause.

Ray   Don't tell the others.

Gilda   I have to –

Ray   You don't have to do anything, and there's nothing *to* downplay because it's nothing, it's nothing to make a fuss about –

Gilda   I have to / take some kind of action –

Ray   No, no, no, no, Don't tell Clarky. Clark. Don't tell him.

Pause.

Ray   Alright?

Gilda   I –

Ray   Don't –

Gilda   *Okay.*

. . .

It's not as if they could – We can't *take* you anywhere, can we.

Beat.

Ray   Embarrassing enough.

. . .

Looking at me the way you did . . .

Gilda   I helped you.

Ray   I don't need you to pity me.

Gilda   Keep your voice down, one of them could walk in any minute.

If that's what you're scared of.

Ray   I don't need your pity.

Gilda   Okay. You don't have it.

Pause.

You have a real –

Ray   What.

Gilda   . . .

You have a real issue with women.

Beat.

Ray   Where do you get that from?

She makes a face.

Ray   I may have an issue with *you* –

Gilda   And what have I ever done to you?

Ray   The whole *planet* has an issue with women –

Gilda   Which planet would that be.

Ray   You want to feel better about how I treat you, just watch any TV show back home and see what people think of women your age.

Gilda   *My* age?

Ray   I'm not prejudiced.

I'm an *astronaut*.

Gilda   The two aren't mutually – And how old do you think I – You're dripping on your photos –

She moves the photos away from the pooling blood.

Ray Don't touch those –

Gilda You're covering them in blood.

She moves them to safety then starts to change his cloth for a clean one.

Pause.

Ray You didn't cry.

Gilda Did you expect me to.

Ray You cry a lot.

Gilda This wasn't such a surprise. With your behaviour recently.

Ray . . .

Pause.

Gilda How will you explain the blood.

Ray I'll clean it.

Gilda What about the cut.

Ray I don't wear short sleeves.

She dabs blood from the photos.

Ray   Be careful with those, they're extremely old.

Gilda   I am – I know – It's your blood.

Pause.

Are these relatives? Ancestors?

Ray   I don't know any of these people.

Gilda   You have pictures of strangers.

Ray   I collect them.

Gilda   You collect old photographs.

Ray   That's very valuable that one –

Gilda   Al*right*.

Ray   . . . It was taken on an early space flight. Nineteen sixties.

. . .

Damn near bankrupted myself getting hold of that one.

Gilda   You can't just look at them online?

Ray   They exist.

No one has anything that *exists* anymore.

Everything you own is just ones and zeroes.

. . .

They have a life.

Light trapped in paper.

Something from then I can hold onto now.

He looks at the photo.

Ray   Back when space travel meant something.

When people cared.

Gilda   Some people still care.

Ray   *No one* cares.

They care so much they've ditched us here and cut off contact.

Gilda   It's a technical fault, they'll fix it.

Ray   And how are you on your history, because we didn't send anyone anywhere for *decades* –

Gilda   We've always launched –

Ray   Not people.

Not people.

The only reason we even *started* way back when was just to fuck Russia.

Beat them to the first rock in spitting distance.

Once we started having our wars with countries that used *sticks* for weapons there was no threat of any of *them* getting out to Mars. Europa.

Gilda   We have people on both now.

Ray   Just your lot.

Scientists. People looking at rocks.

And only since the birds dropped out the trees.

Only to find some way of prolonging whatever paltry existence we can manage on our own planet. The one we *ruined*. It's too *late*.

Gilda   Ray, this isn't –

Ray   All that'll happen next is the rich'll start shipping themselves out to their own private tin cans like this one, on whichever planet they can afford.

And no one gives a damn. Earth is pissing its last and everyone's just looking at their fucking shoes.

Gilda   Ray –

Ray   When I get back they're going to *retire* me, do you understand? They don't give two shits about an old cunt like me –

Gilda   *Ray.*

Ray *catches his breath.*

Pause.

Gilda   If this is what you're worried about I'd have thought you'd be happy with the current situation. Happy enough not to –

Ray   Is anyone waiting for you. Back there.

Beat.

Gilda   No.

Ray   Me either.

. . .

Last run I did I thought about messing with the comms.

Pause.

Gilda   Did you – Are you the reason –

Ray No.

Gilda Did you do something to the –

Ray *No.*

. . .

I said I thought about it, I'm not. . .

. . .

. . .

I'm not like that.

Pause.

Gilda Okay.

Pause.

Ray I used to want to stay out here but the thought of that now, with everything. . .

. . .

Rotting away inside these walls.

. . .

Watching it all stretch out in front of me.

. . .

Can't go back, can't stay here. . .

Gilda You can go back. We're all going back.

Someone will come and get us.

. . .

But I need to know if I need to watch you.

Ray   Hide the knives.

Gilda   I'm serious. Is this a real attempt, or,

. . .

Do we need to have you on watch?

He looks out the window.

Gilda   Ray.

Pause.

Ray.

VII.

Late.

The room is dark, few lights on.

Ray *sits alone, finishing tearing the last of his photographs into pieces.*

He's weeping.

His hand stifles much of the sound as his body wracks with sobs.

We watch him for a while.

Eventually he calms.
Catches his breath.

He looks exhausted.

A fluttering.

A whistle,
A fluttering.

Ray *looks up –*

A fluttering.

There's a bird in here.

It whistles.

Luscinia megarhynchos.

He stands and tries to get near it.

It flutters about the ceiling, looping, circling.

Ray   Hello . . . hello pretty one . . .

He drags a chair closer and stands on it, the bird just out of reach.

Ray   Come on now, come and, don't be shy, come and –

With a whistle the bird swoops up through the access hatch into the space above.

Wait, waitwaitwait . . .

He clambers up the ladder and disappears after it.

We hear fainter whistling, fluttering from above.

Ray (*from above*)   Don't be scared – Don't – Come here with me, come with me –

One of the cupboard doors in the kitchen opens.

A tin can rolls out and across the floor.

The clock glitches and scrambles a little.

More whistling.

Ray (*from above*)   There we are, I got you, I got you, don't worry –

Ray *climbs back down the ladder, clutching his hands together carefully –*

Ray   I got you, I got you.

Don't worry, shhhhhshshshsh –

What a pretty one you are, what a pretty one, eh?

. . .

Let's have a look at you, let's have a little –

He opens his hands very gently but finds them empty.

He looks around the room, the ceiling,

He spots the tin can on the floor.

Picks it up.

There's a rustling coming from the open cupboard.

The clock begins to glitch and scramble more.

*A **Girl** is crawling out into the room backwards.*

Maybe four or five years old.

Ray *drops the can.*

He stares as she emerges.

She stands and turns to face him.

Where her mouth should be, a large X is carved into her face.

She watches him.

He takes a penknife from his pocket and flicks it open.

He stabs it brutally into his neck, over and over and over.

He hacks at the tendons, windpipe, jugular.

Blood cascades down his front in rivers and waves.

He drops the knife and grabs at the gore spilling from his neck.

He turns to the wall and stumbles against it, gurgling, choking, yelping.

He paints a vast, smeared X onto the wall with the colour that pours from him.

Hands slap and drag against the wall.

The clock is frozen on unreadable characters.

The **Girl** *watches.*

Black.

A_ct Two

I.

The same.

The room is messier. More cluttered and dirty.

The clock above the window is frozen on glitched characters.

Gilda *and* **Mattie** *are slumped on the floor.*

Mattie *wears a space suit.*

She vomits into the helmet she cradles between her legs.

Pause.

She spits.

Gilda   Do you want –

Something else.

. . .

To do that in.

Mattie *spits.*

Mattie   I've half-filled it now.

Might as well keep going.

She spits.

Mattie   Does it smell?

Gilda   . . . what?

Mattie *spits.*

Pause.

Mattie   You didn't want to let me in.
Gilda   I thought you were –
Mattie   I scared you. At the window.

Pause.

She spits.

Mattie   It was a long time.
Gilda   We thought everyone had . . .
I stopped believing anyone was coming.

Pause.

Everything stopped working . . .

Pause.

Mattie   The girls – The life systems –
Gilda   They're still . . .
. . .

Mattie   But everything else . . .
The suits all –
We can't get outside anymore.

. . .

And,

We lost all the –

All our computers.

. . .

Everything we had left.

From Earth.

. . .

Everything went.

Beat.

We can't – We don't –

She gestures to the clock.

It stopped.

. . .

Everything stopped.

. . .

. . .

I don't know what it even. . .

Pause.

Mattie   So you don't know how long –

Gilda   Tell me again.

Mattie   . . .

Gilda   Tell me – Start again –

. . .

They *sent* you here.

Pause.

Mattie   I'm here.

Gilda   You're here to take us home.

. . .

Tell me again.

Mattie   I'm here.

Gilda   Can I touch you?

. . .

Just to –

. . .

. . .

To be sure?

Pause.

They reach out across the gap.

They touch.

[   ]

The same.

Gilda, **Cole**, *and* **Clark**.

Gilda *chews her hair.*

Pause.

Cole   Start again.

Clark   I don't get it.

Pause.

Clark   I don't get what you mean.

Cole   Start again.

Gilda   I told you –

Cole   Tell it again. Tell us. Start again.

Pause.

Cole   You're in here.

Pause.

Cole   Start a / *gain* –

Gilda   Al*right*.

. . .

I'm in here. It's,

I'm sitting –

Cole   Where.

Gilda   Just – Here.

Cole   And you see –

Gilda   Don't *prompt* me.

I see her.

Cole   At the window.

Gilda   At the window –

Clark   What's she look like?

Gilda   Like a – Person.

Cole   Like what.

Gilda   Like a person looks.

Small –

Clark   Is she smiling?

Gilda   I can't – I can't see her face because of the – The reflection.

Cole   Then she disappears.

Gilda   She doesn't disappear, she goes, she goes around to the airlock –

Cole   She comes in –

Clark   You let her in?

Gilda   No, I – She –

Cole   She gets in here. She gets inside.

Clark   How come you're in here then?

Gilda   Because I, I back away –

Clark   You're scared.

Gilda   She hasn't taken the helmet off and I back away and I fall,

Cole   And you're in here.

Gilda   And she takes her helmet off and sits and, she's, ah, sick. Into the helmet.

Beat.

Clark   What?

Cole   Why.

Gilda   Because she just landed, she's nauseous, she doesn't feel / well, she –

Clark   She's travel / sick.

Gilda   No –

Cole   Does it smell.

Gilda   What?

Cole   Can you smell it.

Gilda   Why / would I –

Clark   What's that / matter?

Cole   *Can you smell the vomit.*

Gilda   I don't –

No.

I don't know.

You can't remember smells.

Beat.

Clark   It's a weird thing to ask.

Cole   Then what.

Gilda   We're talking. I'm not – I don't say much.

Cole   Why.

Gilda   Because I'm, In shock. I'm just trying to listen, she asks me questions, but I can't get much out, I'm –

Cole   What questions.

Gilda   Where everyone is –

Cole   Where we are.

Clark   Does she know our names?

Gilda   No. Yes. Probably. I guess she does but doesn't say –

Clark   How does she know?

Gilda   Because they *sent* her here.

. . .

Cole   What else.

Gilda   She – She says it's the middle of the day.

Clark   What?

Gilda   She asks where you are and I tell her you're asleep and she says it's the middle of the day. It's strange you're asleep because it's the middle of the day by, by Universal – By their time.

Beat.

Gilda   So I show her the clock and she asks how long it's been like that and I say we can't tell and she says we've been out of contact a long time,

Cole   How long.

Gilda   She didn't say –

Cole   You didn't *ask* her –

Gilda   *No.*

I didn't.

. . .

Alright?

Pause.

Gilda   She asks about Ray.

Clark   About Ray?

Gilda   She asks to see the captain and I tell her.

Clark   What does she / say?

Cole   Does she ask to see the body.

Gilda   No.

Clark   Why would she want to?

Cole   To prove she's not lying.

Clark   Why would she lie?

Gilda   She didn't ask.

. . .

I just told her.

Beat.

Cole   Then what else.

Gilda   Then nothing.

Then you come in and you see her and you ask all the same questions.

Cole   And *what* do we ask.

Gilda   You were th / ere –

Cole   Tell me. You tell me what I asked.

Pause.

Gilda   . . .

You ask her about Earth. You ask her –

You don't ask her name –

You're rude to her.

You're suspicious.

Cole   She *is* suspicious.

Gilda   She's here to take us home.

Cole   Why do they send one person. Why is she alone.

Gilda   She tells you.

Cole   It doesn't make sense.

Gilda   It's expensive.

Clark   They need room in the shuttle to take us home.

Gilda   You don't ask her how long it's been. What the date is.

Cole   She doesn't *tell* us –

Gilda   She just wants to eat.

Cole   And what does she eat.

Gilda   / Cereal.

Clark   Krispy Wows.

Cole   All she wants after six months of travel is cereal.

Clark   What does that matter?

Gilda   She can eat on her ship.

Clark   That's what you're worried about?

Cole   What are we talking about.

Gilda   She wasn't starving –

Cole   What are we *talking* about.

Gilda   Earth.

Cole   *Specifics*.

Clark   Calm down / man –

Gilda   *Trees*.

. . .

. . .

She tells us her tree story.

Pause.

Cole   What tree story.

Clark   I don't remember that.

Pause.

Gilda   She tells us she saw one.

She was with one of the last trees.

When it was dying.

. . .

It's up on the back of a, a truck in this village somewhere, and she's lifted up to touch it, and there's all these men with guns –

Clark That's my story.

Pause.

Gilda What?

Clark That's my story, I told you that.

Pause.

Gilda No, no –

Clark In South America.

Gilda Yes, and the military are all –

Clark This is my story, this happened to me.

Gilda No –

Clark I was six. My uncle lifted me through the crowd. Onto the truck. I touched it.

I told you this.

Gilda . . .

She –

Clark I told you this ages ago, you always wanted to hear hippy stuff like that.

Pause.

Cole Why would she tell you this. The trees died decades before we got here.

It's not news.

Beat.

Clark   I was six.

Pause.

Gilda   . . .

Stop looking at me like that –

Cole   What's wrong with you.

Gilda   Nothing's *wrong* with me –

Cole   Then why –

Gilda   Maybe I'm just confused because, she was,

she was talking about Earth, and you were talking about Earth,

It's not –

It's not indicative of anything like you're –

. . .

Stop *staring* at me.

. . .

. . .

You're asking me all these questions and they're all,

And it's not –

It doesn't *mean* anything.

. . .

. . .

. . .

Yes, okay, maybe I do remember you told me,

I just got it –

I got muddled with the,

or maybe I heard it from the girl who used to manage life systems,

maybe you told her and she told me and that's how I, I –

It doesn't matter, what matters is –

Clark   What girl.

Gilda   Fuck *off*.

Cole   *He* manages life systems. He's tech. *What* girl.

Pause.

Gilda   This must have been a different, another –

Cole   You said it was your first time out here.

Gilda   I know –

Cole   You never worked off-world before.

Gilda   I *know*.

Cole   So then *what*.

Pause.

Cole   What are you *saying*.

Gilda   We had a –

. . .

. . .

I –

. . .

. . .

She was *here*. We talked a lot. She liked to hear about the
past –

She was the one Ray told about the, the things he was seeing,
she told me about Ray's –

Clark   I told you that.

Gilda   Stop it!

Clark   Ray told *me* about the girl at the window, *I* told you, *I*
told you that.

Pause.

Gilda   . . .

Cole   She's gone.

Gilda   I'm not –

Cole   She's lost it.

Gilda   Don't *fucking* talk about me like I'm not here – I'm
here, / I'm –

Cole   The last person who started seeing girls who weren't
there opened his throat on the walls.

Clark   Leave her alone, it doesn't mean she's –

Gilda   I don't need you to defend me, I am not – I can –
Whatever you're –

Cole   How many people on our crew.

Gilda   What?

Cole   Including Ray. How many.

Gilda   Four.

Cole   Four. One, two, three, and one in the freezer.

Where's this extra girl.

Pause.

Cole   One two three, one in the freezer.

Where's the fifth.

Where's this extra person.

Who *is* this person.

Gilda   . . . she was –

Cole   *What*.

Gilda   How do I know that it's not –

That *you* both forgot, or, or that you're both just *saying* this to, / to –

Clark   I wouldn't do that to / you . . .

Cole   You're talking with *ghosts*.

Gilda   I'm not – I don't – And if I am then so are you, you *both* talked to her –

Cole   Who. Which one. There's two now, which one did we talk to?

Gilda   The *one* – The one from *Earth*. They sent her to take us home, you *saw* her.

Talked to her. You *said* –

Cole   So where *is* she.

Gilda   She said, you saw, I told you, she went out on the surface, / she's outside, she –

Clark   Let's maybe, we / should maybe chill our boots here –

Cole   You told us –

Gilda   This morning –

Cole   How do you know when morning was?

Clark   / I don't think this is a good –

Gilda   She's *here*.

Cole   Where? And how did she *get* here.

Gilda   A ship, a shuttle, a, a,

Cole   Have you seen it.

Gilda   . . .

Cole   Did you see what she supposedly arrived in.

Beat.

They both rush to the window and scan the surface.

Clark   Let's just all take a / sec and –

Cole   *Where.*

Gilda   Check the – It'll be on the other side –

They hurry off, **Cole** *orders* **Clark** –

Cole   Check that side, you check that side –

They split.

Pause.

They come back on. **Cole** *limps heavily from now on.*

Gilda   No?

Clark (*shakes head*)   No.

Gilda *rushes to check* **Clark**'s *side.*

Clark   Maybe we can't see though, it's further away –

Cole   There's nothing there.

Gilda *comes back.*

Clark   She left already –

Cole   We didn't notice?

Clark   We were sleeping,

Gilda   It'll be out there somewhere, we just –

Cole   It never happened. She was never here.

Beat.

Gilda   You *saw* her.

Cole   There's no one here. It's a mirage.

Gilda   You can't *touch* a mirage –

Mirages don't talk.

Mirages don't eat *cereal* –

They *sent* someone.

. . .

. . .

You saw her, didn't you.

You saw her.

Beat.

Clark   . . . I mean . . . I think I did . . .

Cole   You didn't see anything.

Clark   I can – Sort of – *Feel* it. I feel like I saw someone.

Cole   She's telling you your own stories.

Gilda   That wasn't –

Cole   She told us some fiction and enough time's passed that she's convinced us it's fact.

Gilda   That's ludicrous –

Cole   She's implanted a false memory, / she drilled us –

Gilda   How would I – That's impossible –

Cole   She's convinced us that something that never happened happened.

Gilda   Why would I do that?

Cole   Because you're *insane.*

. . .

. . .

Do you even think this is the first time we've had this argument?

Pause.

Gilda   You *saw* her . . .

. . .

You said, you both said, you both – You *talked* to her –

Cole   Don't talk to me anymore.

Gilda   You don't get to *diagnose* me –

Cole   The more she says the more at risk we are –

Gilda   If I am what you're – Then so are you, so are *both* of you, I'm not making up people who aren't *there* –

Cole   Stop talking –

Gilda   Whatever's happening is happening to you too, it's –

Cole   Shut *up* –

He grabs at her throat and face, forcing her to the floor –

Cole   / Shut *up*, shut your *mouth* –

Clark   Hey –!

Gilda   / Get *off* me –

Cole   Help me with her, *help* me with her –

Clark *wrestles* **Cole** *away –* **Gilda** *manages to squirm out of his grip.*

Clark   What's *wrong* with you?

Cole   She is *dangerous*, she is *delusional* –

Clark   You're acting like a fucking maniac –

Cole   This has to be fixed *now*. She is putting our sanity at risk which is putting our *lives* at risk. She is dragging us into her own psychotic world, and I will not let her jeopardise our entire perception of what's –

My *daughter* is waiting for me.

Gilda   Son, you have a son Cole –

Cole   *Whatever she is*, I don't have to –

. . .

What is this –

Why am I –

. . .

. . .

Why am I walking like this?

Pause.

Cole   What's wrong with me.

Gilda *and* **Clark** *look to each other.*

Cole   What.

. . .

What have you *done* to me.

Gilda   No one's done anything to you –

Clark   You forgot again.

Gilda   Clark –

Cole   Forgot what.

. . .

Forgot *what*.

Beat.

Clark   You always tell him better than I do –

Cole   Tell me *what*.

. . .

What are you –

Gilda   It's cancer.

Pause.

You have can / cer –

Cole   You shut your *cunt* mouth Gilda, you, *you* tell me –

. . .

You tell me what this is, I don't trust her, I don't –
You tell me.

Beat.

Clark   We keep telling you –

Cole   You never told me anything –

Clark   You keep forgetting.

. . .

We tell you then you, you forget again.

. . .

I'm sorry.

Cole   . . .

. . .

You don't,
You don't *forget* something like that.

. . .

How do you *forget* that you –

That you're. . .

. . .

You're lying to me, you're with her, you're both, you're trying to make me believe that I'm –

Gilda   Why are you walking like that?

Beat.

Cole   . . . what.

Clark   What's with your leg?

Gilda   Why are you limping.

Cole   I'm . . .

Clark   You sleep on it weird?

Cole   It's nothing –

. . .

There's nothing wrong with me –

Gilda   It's probably nothing.

Clark   Let her scan it so you can shut up about it –

Cole   No –

Gilda   It's a tumour.

Cole   Stop it –

Gilda   I'm sorry.

Clark   You forgot again –

Cole   Stop doing this – Stop it –

Gilda   I'm sorry. Do you remember?

Clark   We scanned you mate, remember?

Cole   What have you done to me –

Gilda   No one's done anything to you –

Clark   You forgot again.

Gilda   You keep forgetting –

Cole   You shut your *cunt* mouth Gilda, you, you tell me –

Clark   You always tell him better than I do –

Cole   *You* tell me.

Gilda   You have a tumour.

Clark   It's cancer.

Gilda   It's wrapped round the base of your spine. It's affecting your movement.

You keep forgetting.

Cole   You don't *forget* – You don't *forget* / something like that –

Gilda   It's a tumour.

Clark   He forgot again –

Cole   How long did I –

Gilda   We just did the scan.

Clark   You remember, don't you mate.

Gilda   It's cancer –

Clark   It's your turn to tell him.

Cole   Tell me *what*?

Gilda   It's wrapped round your spine.

Cole   You shut your *mouth* –

Clark   You've known for ages, mate.

Gilda   I'm sorry –

Cole   It's *nothing* –

Gilda   Cole –

Cole   I'm *fine* –

Gilda   Just let us –

Cole   You're / the ones –

Clark   It's cancer.

Gilda   It's wrapped round your spine.

Cole   No, nononono/ nonono –

Gilda   / I'm sorry.

Clark   Why can't he / remember?

Gilda   Let us scan it –

Clark   You keep forgetting.

Gilda   It spread.

Cole   / Both of you stop talking to me –

Gilda   It's spreading –

Clark   It's wrapped round your spine.

Cole   Cut it –

Gilda   We don't have the facilities to –

Cole   Cut it *out of* / *me* –

Gilda   / Cole –

Clark   Calm down –

Gilda   I'm sorry –

Cole   YOU'RE LYING TO ME.

Gilda   It's wrapped round your spine there's nothing we can do –

Clark   He's gone again –

Cole   You don't get to *tell* me this –

Clark   His ear's going again –

Cole's *ear is bleeding.*

Gilda   Cole –

Cole   What's wrong with me? What is this?

Gilda   Cole –

Cole   Why am I walking like this –

Gilda   I'm sorry –

Cole   *Tell* me.

Clark   He's gone / again.

Gilda   Cole.

Cole   You stay away / from me –

Clark   Can he hear us?

Gilda   / Cole –

Clark   Cole –

Cole   Make them come / get me.

Gilda   Cole –

Cole   You make them come and / get me – Call them, radio them, *fix* it –

Clark   Cole –

Cole *collapses.*

Clark He's gone / again –

Gilda He's out of bed again –

Cole you're doing this to me . . .

Gilda Now / come on,

Clark Come on / mate –

Cole . . . stop doing this to me . . .

Gilda Can you hear us?

Clark He's pissed himself again –

Gilda Don't –

Cole what's wrong with my legs . . .

Gilda Cole –

Clark He's out of bed again –

Gilda You're sick –

Clark You're poorly mate –

Gilda You're not well –

You need to rest –

Are you tired?

Cole stop talking to me like that –

i'm not a –

He vomits.

what is this –

Gilda You're on drugs to make you better –

Clark Are you tired mate?

Gilda Let's go back to bed.

Cole   stop it . . .

Clark *picks up* **Cole**. **Cole** *struggles.*

Clark   It's alright –
Cole   slow it down, stop, stop it, stop making it . . .
Gilda   You just need to sleep –
Clark   You'll feel better tomorrow –
Gilda   Don't say that to him.
Cole   *Stop it*. MAKE IT STOP.

They carry **Cole** *off to his room.*

We hear gabbling, wails, moans.

Clark *comes back on, unsettled.*

A silence.

Pause.

Gilda *comes back in.*

Pause.

Clark   . . . Is he in the freezer now.

Gilda   Yes, but don't . . .

Don't think about that.

Pause.

Clark   How long do you think it was?

Gilda   . . . I don't know.

Clark   . . . Do you –

Do you think it was months, or *years* –

Gilda   I don't know.

Pause.

Clark   He just lay there the whole time, and we couldn't
even –

Gilda   We did the best we could.

. . .

We couldn't –

. . .

We did what we could.

Pause.

Clark   He was a good captain.

Pause.

Gilda He was / n't –

Clark He was the –

Gilda He wasn't the captain.

. . .

He was a meteorologist.

Clark . . .

Gilda He was a scientist. Like me.

Clark . . . Yeah.

. . .

. . .

That's what I – I meant.

. . .

Pause.

Gilda Are you alright?

Pause.

Clark I don't know.

. . .

. . .

I can't . . .

. . .

I really feel like I'm hanging on by my nails here –

How long have you been standing there?

Gilda   You're okay –

Clark   I can't even tell if –

Gilda   We'll do it together.

Clark   . . .

Gilda   We can help each other.

Clark   . . .

Gilda   Okay?

. . .

Start again.

Clark   I don't get it.

Gilda   Start again.

Clark   I don't get what you mean –

Gilda   Start again.

Clark   I told you –

Gilda   Tell it again. Tell me.

Pause.

Gilda   You're in here.

Pause.

Clark   I'm in here. It's – I'm sitting –

. . .

. . .

I see her at the window.

Gilda   What's she look like.

Clark   Like a – Person.

Gilda   Small –

Clark   Like a person looks.

Gilda   Is she smiling?

Clark   I can't see because of the – Reflection –

Gilda   Then she disappears.

Clark   She comes in –

Gilda   You let her in.

Clark   No, I – She –

Gilda   She gets in here,

Clark   I back away –

Gilda   You're scared.

Clark   I back away and fall,

Gilda   And you're in here.

Pause.

Clark   No.

Gilda   No?

Clark   No, that's not – That wasn't –

That wasn't mine.

Pause.

Gilda   How about –

Clark   Start again.

Gilda   I have a ball.

Clark   A ball.

Gilda   I have a ball and you're working.

Clark   I'm doing maths.

Gilda   I'm bored.

Clark   I need –

Gilda   I don't like things that aren't real.

Clark   I'm limping.

Gilda   You're limping.

Clark   My name is . . .

Gilda   X

Clark   I'm . . .

. . .

No.

Gilda   Maths is for –

Clark   No it's, this isn't –

Gilda   I get further away.

Clark   She gets further away.

Gilda   I have a son

Clark   Daughter

Gilda   Who is . . .

Clark   X

Gilda years

Clark Further away

Gilda To always make me tell

Clark X

Gilda For *years*

Clark leaving

Gilda You need a

Clark Computer science.

Gilda Calculator

Clark Left

Gilda X

Clark X

Pause.

Clark Carrr . . .

Gilda Carl –

Clark C – Cl – Cllarr –

Gilda X

Clark X

Gilda Co –

Clark Coa –

Gilda Coast –

Clark Coarse –

Gilda Claw –

Clark Claws –

Gilda   X

Clark   X

Gilda   And the algorithm –

Clark   Watch

Gilda   Rain

Clark   Rain

Gilda   Rail

Clark   X

Gilda   And

– I'm in here

– It's

– I'm

– X

– at the window

– See

– X

– at the

– X

– at

– the girls

– she

– nothing

– mymother

– left

– *No.*

– X

– No.

– . . .

– . . .

– Start again –

– I'm in

– She

– X

– and

– all the –

– X

– X

– hear

– X

– not

– Where

– X

– Enough to

– lift

– X

– Punch the

– X

– crowd

– X

– X

– X

– X

– She

– South America

– South America

– South Amer

– South America

– she's

– X

– One the last

– pillarwebs

– Two

– She's

– X

– One in the freezer

– X in the freezer

– *Two* in the freezer –

– Two in the South Amer

– X

– in the fr

– X

– And

– And

– Birds

– Bird

– Birds

– X

– brush

– brushing

– brush against the

– X

– X

– X

– . . .

– . . .

– Glll –

– Glarr –

– X

– Luscin –

– Glllaah –

– Luscina –

– X

– Lus –

– Glll –

– G –

– G –

– da

– daaaaa

– X

– X

– X / X X X X X X X

– X X X X X X X X / X X X

– Everything

– X

– hold onto X

– hold onto / X in particu X she

– X X X X

– X X X X X X / X X X X X X X X X X X X X X X X X

– X X X X X X X X X X X X X X X X / X X X X

– X X X X X / X X X X X X X X X X X X / X

– X

– X / X

– X

– X

X X X X X X X X X X X X X X X X X X X X X X X X X X
X X X X X X X X X X X X X X X X X X X X X X X X X X
X X X X X X X X X X X X X X X X X X X X X X X X X X
X X X X X X X X X X X X X X X X X X X X X X X X X X
X X X X X X X X X X X X X X X X X X X X X X X X X X
X X X X X X X X X X X X X X X X X X X X X X X X X X
X X X X X X X X X X X X X X X X X X X X X X X X X X
X X X X X X X X X X X X X X X X X X X X X X X X X X
X X X X X X X X X X X X X X X X X X X X X X X X X X
X X X X X X X X X X X X X X X X X X X X X X X X X X
X X X X X X X X X X X X X X X X X X X X X X X X X X
X X X X X X X X X X X X X X X X X X X X X X X X X X
X X X X X X X X X X X X X X X X X X X X X X X X X X
X X X X X X X X X X X X X X X X X X X X X X X X X X
X X X X X X X X X X X X X X X X X X X X X X X X X X
X X X X X X X X X X X X X X X X X X X X X X X X X X

X X X X X X X X X X X X X X X X X X X X X X X X X X X X
X X X X X X X X X X X X X X X X X X X X X X X X X X X X
X X X X X X X X X X X X X X X X X X X X X X X X X X X X
X X X X X X X X X X X X X X X X X X X X X X X X X X X X
X X X X X X X X X X X X X X X X X X X X X X X X X X X X
X X X X X X X X X X X X X X X X X X X X X X X X X X X X
X X X X X X X X X X X X X X X X X X X X X X X X X X X X
X X X X X X X X X X X X X X X X X X X X X X X X X X X X
X X X X X X X X X X X X X X X X X X X X X X X X X X X X
X X X X X X X X X X X X X X X X X X X X X X X X X X X X
X X X X X X X X X X X X X X X X X X X X X X X X X X X X
X X X X X X X X X X X X X X X X X X X X X X X X X X X X
X X X X X X X X X X X X X X X X X X X X X X X X X X X X
X X X X X X X X X X X X X X X X X X X X X X X X X X X X
X X X X X X X X X X X X X X X X X X X X X X X X X X X X
X X X X X X X X X X X X X X X X X X X X X X X X X X X X
X X X X X X X X X X X X X X X X X X X X X X X X X X X X
X X X X X X X X X X X X X X X X X X X X X X X X X X X X
X X X X X X X X X X X X X X X X X X X X X X X X X X X X
X X X X X X X X X X X X X X X X X X X X X X X X X X X X
X X X X X X X X X X X X X X X X X X X X X X X X X X X X
X X X X X X X X X X X X X X X X X X X X X X X X X X X X
X X X X X X X X X X X X X X X X X X X X X X X X X X X X
X X X X X X X X X X X X X X X X X X X X X X X X X X X X
X X X X X X X X X X X X X X X X X X X X X X X X X X X X
X X X X X X X X X X X X X X X X X X X X X X X X X X X X
X X X X X X X X X X X X X X X X X X X X X X X X X X X X
X X X X X X X X X X X X X X X X X X X X X X X X X X X X
X X X X X X X X X X X X X X X X X X X X X X X X X X X X
X X X X X X X X X X X X X X X X X X X X X X X X X X X X
X X X X X X X X X X X X X X X X X X X X X X X X X X X X
X X X X X X X X X X X X X X X X X X X X X X X X X X X X
X X X X X X X X X X X X X X X X X X X X X X X X X X X X
X X X X X X X X X X X X X X X X X X X X X X X X X X X X
X X X X X X X X X X X X X X X X X X X X X X X X X X X X
X X X X X X X X X X X X X X X X X X X X X X X X X X X X
X X X X X X X X X X X X X X X X X X X X X X X X X X X X

X X X X X X X X X X X X X X X X X X X X X X X X X X X
X X X X X X X X X X X X X X X X X X X X X X X X X X X
X X X X X X X X X X X X X X X X X X X X X X X X X X X
X X X X X X X X X X X X X X X X X X X X X X X X X X X
X X X X X X X X X X X X X X X X X X X X X X X X X X X
X X X X X X X X X X X X X X X X X X X X X X X X X X X
X X X X X X X X X X X X X X X X X X X X X X X X X X X
X X X X X X X X X X X X X X X X X X X X X X X X X X X
X X X X X X X X X X X X X X X X X X X X X X X X X X X
X X X X X X X X X X X X X X X X X X X X X X X X X X X
X X X X X X X X X X X X X X X X X X X X X X X X X X X
X X X X X X X X X X X X X X X X X X X X X X X X X X X
X X X X X X X X X X X X X X X X X X X X X X X X X X X
X X X X X X X X X X X X X X X X X X X X X X X X X X X
X X X X X X X X X X X X X X X X X X X X X X X X X X X
X X X X X X X X X X X X X X X X X X X X X X X X X X X
X X X X X X X X X X X X X X X X X X X X X X X X X X X
X X X X X X X X X X X X X X X X X X X X X X X X X X X
X X X X X X X X X X X X X X X X X X X X X X X X X X X
X X X X X X X X X X X X X X X X X X X X X X X X X X X
X X X X X X X X X X X X X X X X X X X X X X X X X X X
X X X X X X X X X X X X X X X X X X X X X X X X X X X
X X X X X X X X X X X X X X X X X X X X X X X X X X X
X X X X X X X X X X X X X X X X X X X X X X X X X X X
X X X X X X X X X X X X X X X X X X X X X X X X X X X
X X X X X X X X X X X X X X X X X X X X X X X X X X X
X X X X X X X X X X X X X X X X X X X X X X X X X X X
X X X X X X X X X X X X X X X X X X X X X X X X X X X
X X X X X X X X X X X X X X X X X X X X X X X X X X X
X X X X X X X X X X X X X X X X X X X X X X X X X X X
X X X X X X X X X X X X X X X X X X X X X X X X X X X
X X X X X X X X X X X X X X X X X X X X X X X X X X X
X X X X X X X X X X X X X X X X X X X X X X X X X X X
X X X X X X X X X X X X X X X X X X X X X X X X X X X
X X X X X X X X X X X X X X X X X X X X X X X X X X X
X X X X X X X X X X X X X X X X X X X X X X X X X X X

X X X X X X X X X X X X X X X X X X X X X X X X X
X X X X X X X X X X X X X X X X X X X X X X X X X
X X X X X X X X X X X X X X X X X X X X X X X X X
X X X X X X X X X X X X X X X X X X X X X X X X X
X X X X X X X X X X X X X X X X X X X X X X X X X
X X X X X X X X X X X X X X X X X X X X X X X X X
X X X X X X X X X X X X X X X X X X X X X X X X X
X X X X X X X X X X X X X X X X X X X X X X X X X
X X X X X X X X X X X X X X X X X X X X X X X X X
X X X X X X X X X X X X X X X X X X X X X X X X X
X X X X X X X X X X X X X X X X X X X X X X X X X
X X X X X X X X X X X X X X X X X X X X X X X X X
X X X X X X X X X X X X X X X X X X X X X X X X X
X X X X X X X X X X X X X X X X X X X X X X X X X
X X X X X X X X X X X X X X X X X X X X X X X X X
X X X X X X X X X X X X X X X X X X X X X X X X X
X X X X X X X X X X X X X X X X X X X X X X X X X
X X X X X X X X X X X X X X X X X X X X X X X X X
X X X X X X X X X X X X X X X X X X X X X X X X X
X X X X X X X X X X X X X X X X X X X X X X X X X
X X X X X X X X X X X X X X X X X X X X X X X X X
X X X X X X X X X X X X X X X X X X X X X X X X X
X X X X X X X X X X X X X X X X X X X X X X X X X
X X X X X X X X X X X X X X X X X X X X X X X X X
X X X X X X X X X X X X X X X X X X X X X X X X X
X X X X X X X X X X X X X X X X X X X X X X X X X
X X X X X X X X X X X X X X X X X X X X X X X X X
X X X X X X X X X X X X X X X X X X X X X X X X X
X X X X X X X X X X X X X X X X X X X X X X X X X
X X X X X X X X X X X X X X X X X X X X X X X X X
X X X X X X X X X X X X X X X X X X X X X X X X X
X X X X X X X X X X X X X X X X X X X X X X X X X
X X X X X X X X X X X X X X X X X X X X X X X X X
X X X X X X X X X X X X X X X X X X X X X X X X X
X X X X X X X X X X X X X X X X X X X X X X X X X
X X X X X X X X X X X X X X X X X X X X X X X X X

X X X X X X X X X X X X X X X X X X X X X X X X X
X X X X X X X X X X X X X X X X X X X X X X X X X
X X X X X X X X X X X X X X X X X X X X X X X X X
X X X X X X X X X X X X X X X X X X X X X X X X X

X

X

− . . .

− . . .

− X

− . . .

− . . .

− And I'm

− . . .

− X

− . . .

− . . .

− . . .

− . . .

− And I'm in here −

− I'm in

− X

– . . .

– . . .

– I'm

– . . .

– . . .

– . . .

Clark How long do you think.

Gilda I don't know. Even if we knew, we wouldn't know.

Clark . . . Just *waiting* . . .

Gilda Just like always.

Clark Waiting to die.

Gilda Don't say that.

– . . .

Clark It's been forever.

Gilda We don't know that.

Clark No one's ever going to come.

They're all gone. We're the last.

Gilda You're being –

Clark I just wish we knew. Then we could punch our cards right now –

Gilda That's enough.

Clark You should just put me in the freezer –

Gilda Stop it now.

Clark . . . with the others . . .

Gilda Come on. I can't talk to you if you're going to start blubbing every time –

Clark I'm not.

. . .

I'm not blubbing.

. . .

And if I was it'd be. . .

. . .

I'm allowed.

Gilda   Is it because you thought you heard a ghost.

Clark   I don't think I heard a ghost –

Gilda   There's no such thing as ghosts.

Clark   I know.

Gilda   It's just the girls.

Clark   The girls. Yeah.

Gilda   Why don't we play a game or something.

Clark   I wish you could tell me who I was.

Gilda   You know who you are.

Gilda   You know who you are.

Clark   I wish I'd done lots of things different.

Gilda   That's normal. You can't . . .

That's okay.

Clark   . . . I wish I'd held my farts in more around you.

Gilda   Well. You can start now.

Clark   i'm leaving you all alone.

Clark   you'll be all on your own out here.

that's the worst . . .

Clark   i thought i could hold on longer.

. . .

but i can't.

. . .

i'm sputtering out.

. . .

my body's catching up with my brain.

Gilda   It's alright.

Clark   i don't want to leave you out here on your own, i can't –

Gilda   I don't need you to look after me.

I'll be fine.

. . .

You just worry about yourself.

Clark   what about my name.

Gilda   What about it?

Clark   . . .

Gilda   We can have new names.

Clark   . . . like what.

Gilda   Well. It can be anything you want.

Clark   . . .

. . .

Kratos.

Gilda   Okay.

Okay Kratos.

Gilda   Are you warm enough.

Clark   . . . no.

Gilda   How about now.

Clark   did i kiss you once?

Gilda   Yes. More than once.

Clark   i thought maybe –

Gilda   No. That was real.

Clark   . . . can i do it again?

Clark   that was nice.

Gilda   Yes.

Clark   i thought maybe i'd . . .

. . .

you laughed at my jokes.

Gilda   Some of them.

Clark   eventually.

. . .

i always fancied you.

. . .

i won you round.

Gilda   Alright. Don't gloat.

Clark   i'm so sorry . . .

Gilda   Shush now.

Clark   i'm sorry.

Gilda   Just try and sleep.

Clark   maybe they'll come

Gilda   Maybe.

Maybe when you wake up they'll be here.

. . .

But either way I'll definitely be here.

. . .

I'm here.

. . .

You can count on me.

Kratos.

Clark   all this time.

Clark   all this time i thought i was the main character.

Clark   x . . .
Gilda   X.
Clark   xo . . .

Gilda XO.

I
Gilda *is alone.*

II
Gilda *is alone.*

III
Gilda *is alone.*
She stands by the window looking out into the black.

IV
Gilda *sees herself standing by the window.*

V
A bed stands by the window where the second **Gilda** *was,*
a blanket covering a form beneath it.
Gilda *watches as the form thrashes through a violent seizure.*

VI
Clark *and* **Cole** *eat cereal at the table.*
Gilda *is fixed to the bed.*
She struggles and shouts for their attention but no sound comes from
her.

VII
Ray *and* **Mattie** *eat cereal at the table.*
Ray *feeds his spoon into the ragged gash in his neck, milk and blood*
streaming out.
Gilda *kicks and bucks in the bed, which seems to be swallowing her.*
She screams silently in desperation.

VIII
Gilda *cowers against a wall.*
A gigantic nightingale lies on the floor, injured, bleeding.
Gilda *appears the size of an infant next to it.*
She shrinks from the bird's laboured breathing.
Hands begin to push from within the bird's chest,
a swallowed figure wrestling out from within the flesh.

IX
The machinery, the life systems, all have increased in volume tenfold.
Gilda *crouches on all fours howling in agony.*
The sound is deafening.
The walls run thick with blood.

The light slowly returns to the room.

Gilda *is still crouched on the floor.*

She tries to catch her breath.

The cupboard door under the sink swings open.

A tin can rolls out.

Gilda *watches as the* **Girl** *crawls out into the room backwards.*

She stands and turns around.

Her face is unscarred.

They consider each other.

Girl   You didn't find me.

Pause.

Gilda   No.

Pause.

Girl   Do you give up?

Gilda *nods*.

Girl   I was just in there. I hid in there.
Gilda   Yes.

Pause.

Girl   Well what is – What you have to – If you don't *find* me, then you have to, you have to do it again.

Because you didn't win.

Gilda   Okay –

Girl   And that's because you didn't find me again when I was up the ladder. I was up in there and you didn't find me as well.

Gilda   No.

Girl   So you just, Just wait here and, and you have to count again and you can't look.

Gilda   Okay –

Girl   Just don't look then, don't look!

She runs to hide –

Gilda   I – No – Wait – *Mattie.*

She stops.

Pause.

I can't . . .

. . .

I don't want to play this now.

. . .

I like to –

. . .

I like to know where you are.

Pause.

Young Mattie   Are you sad again?
Gilda   No, I'm –
I'm okay –

Young Mattie *goes and sits on* **Gilda** *heavily.*

Gilda   Oof –
Young Mattie   Why are you?
Gilda   I'm not, I'm fine, I'm –
Young Mattie   You're crying.

Gilda   I'm just – Don't do that please –

Young Mattie *is pressing her thumbs on* **Gilda**'s *eyes*.

Gilda   I just got mixed up.

I'm fine now I can see you.

Young Mattie   When can we play again though?

. . .

When I'm older?

Gilda   Maybe.

Pause.

Young Mattie   How old am I now do you think?

Pause.

Gilda   I don't know sweetheart.

. . .

Pause.

How old do you think I am?

Young Mattie   . . . Old. Really old.

Gilda   That's nice.

Young Mattie   Very old.

Gilda   Thank you.

Well why don't we measure ourselves, that'll tell us something.

Young Mattie   Yes!

She runs over to one of the walls and stands excitedly against it –

Young Mattie   I can see – It's bigger!

Gilda   Where's your pencil.

Young Mattie   It's in the –

Gilda   We can't mark it without a pencil, can we.

Young Mattie   You just – You just keep your hand where it's – Where how tall I am is –

Gilda   I – Okay –

Young Mattie   Hold it really still though –

Gilda   Please.

Young Mattie   Please –

She dashes from the room.

Pause.

Gilda *looks at the pencil marks.*

Gilda   I don't need to –

. . .

We can just measure you again.

. . .

Mattie.

Pause.

She removes her hand.

She seems exhausted.

She pushes her hands through her hair, which greys as she does so, colour ebbing away.

Pause.

Mattie *comes in, an adult again*

She's brought pillows and blankets to set up a makeshift bed by the window.

Mattie   Mum.

Gilda   . . .

Mattie   What?

Gilda   . . . I thought you were in there.

. . .

Mattie   I'm in here.

Gilda   I thought I heard someone . . .

. . .

What's all this?

Mattie   You said you wanted to be by the window.

Gilda   . . .

Mattie   Didn't you.

Gilda   . . .

Mattie   Mum.

Gilda   Did you bring the pencil?

Mattie   The pencil –?

Gilda   To say how old you are.

Mattie   I – Yes. We did that.

Gilda   You saw how old?

Mattie   I did.

Gilda   You're always asking me.

Mattie   I know. Let's –

Gilda   I'm going to work out in space you know.

Mattie   Yes –

Gilda   I'm going to work off-world. I always wanted to.

Mattie   You did.

Gilda   Since I was tiny.

Mattie   Come lie down for a bit.

Gilda *goes and gets into bed.*

Gilda   Just be careful when you're out there.

Mattie   I will.

Gilda   And call me.

Mattie   Okay.

Gilda   I know you're busy but there's always time to call.

Mattie   There is. How's that? Warm enough?

Gilda   Are we still waiting?

Mattie   No, we're not waiting for anything.

Gilda   We're not?

Mattie   No.

Gilda   Oh.

. . .

Pause.

I don't know what time it is even.

. . .

And I can't see anything out this window.

. . .

I'm so useless aren't I.

Mattie   Course not –

Gilda   And I'm always *crying* –

Mattie   That's okay.

Gilda   It's pathetic.

Mattie   It's allowed.

Pause.

Gilda   I just thought –

I'd always have enough time.

To say all the things I wanted to say to you.

Mattie   You don't need to –

Gilda   I just wanted to tell you that I love you.

With *everything*.

Mattie   I know.

Gilda   It's so much it's the only thing that's left.

. . .

I can't remember half of anything but you're in all of it.

You're in everything.

All jumbled around.

. . .

. . .

And I was selfish.

Mattie   Why?

Gilda   Because.

I had you so I wouldn't be alone.

Mattie   That's alright –

Gilda   But I'm leaving you here –

Mattie   It's okay –

Gilda   You came to rescue me and I'm leaving you here –

Mattie   Ssshh . . .

Gilda   I don't want to leave you out here on your own, I can't bear it –

Mattie   I'll be fine.

. . .

You just –

Worry about yourself.

. . .

. . .

Come on, I can't talk to you if you're blubbing all the time, can I?

Gilda   I'm not blubbing.

Mattie   No.

Me either.

Pause.

Gilda   I'm tired.

Mattie   I know.

Gilda   So tired all the time.

Mattie   Well don't go to sleep yet. Stay up and talk to me.

. . .

Tell me what it was like back there. Before.

Gilda   You make me tell all that too much.

Mattie   Alright, then –

Gilda   And I can't remember it all.

Mattie   Well then tell me about my father.

Gilda (*mock serious voice*)   Your *father* . . .

Mattie   What was he like.

Gilda   I told you all that too.

Mattie   Well tell me again.

Gilda   . . .

He was annoying.

Mattie   Annoying?

Gilda   Very annoying.

And rude. And stupid.

. . .

More daft than stupid.

Mattie   But you loved him.

Gilda   Eventually.

I came around.

. . .

He was very scared.

. . .

He was scared I'd go first.

Pause.

Mattie   Mum –

Gilda   Mattie!

Mattie   Wh –

Gilda   Mattie –

Mattie   I'm here, I'm –

Young Mattie *comes in.*

Young Mattie   I'm here.

Gilda   Did you do your teeth?

Young Mattie   Yes.

Gilda   If I give your mouth a sniff is it going to smell fresh?

Young Mattie   I did them!

Gilda   Okay then.

Mattie   / I'm still . . .

Young Mattie   Can I sleep with you?

Gilda   I thought you liked your own bed.

Young Mattie (*shrugs*)   Only sometimes.

Gilda   Only sometimes. Alright.

Young Mattie *clambers into bed.*

Gilda   You warm enough?

Young Mattie   No . . .

Gilda   How about now. That's better isn't it.

Young Mattie   Yes.

Gilda   Yes.

Mattie   yes . . .

Pause.

Young Mattie   Mum?

Gilda   What?

Young Mattie   What was your mum like?

Gilda   You make me tell all that too much.

Young Mattie   I like it though.

Gilda   I'm too tired now.

Young Mattie   Please.

Pause.

Mattie   please . . .

Beat.

Gilda   My mother.
Was the last tree.

Beat.

Young Mattie   / What did she look like?
Mattie   what did she look like.
Gilda   Big. Tall. She brushed against the sky.
She was filled with the most brilliant colour and light.
People came from all around to see her.
To hear her speak for the past.

. . .

And everyone would listen and listen, and cry and cry.
They'd ask every question they could think to ask.
And cry for what she told them.
For how things used to be.

. . .

Until eventually she couldn't speak anymore.
The colour and light faded.
And her leaves turned to dust.

. . .

So with her very last breath,
She lifted me here.

Away from what was left.

Sent to remember the rest.

. . .

. . .

. . . are you asleep?

. . .

Mattie   . . . no . . .

Gilda *kisses her daughter goodnight.*

Gilda   Sleep tight.

Pause.

Mattie   . . . mum . . .

. . .

i'm still awake . . .

. . .

i'm still here . . .

. . .

. . .

i'm here . . .

. . .

i'm here . . .

. . .

i'm here . . .

. . .

i'm here . . .

. . .

i'm here . . .

As she repeats, we start to hear the ambient sound of a forest.

The birds sing and whistle to each other.

Then –

Black.

Notes

Nothing at all is visible out the window.

The clock above the window should run normally throughout each scene in Act One with the exception of **V** and **X**, where the glitches and breaks are marked.

In Act Two, Clark wears Ray's watch throughout.

Nothing should underline when time is speeding up, shifting, etc. The shifts in the dialogue are the only clues.

The nine short scenes found in Act Two should last longer than they perhaps appear to on the page.